Simple Prayers
& Blessings

MARGARET ANNE HUFFMAN

GARY WILDE

Publications International, Ltd.

ISBN: 0-7853-2826-2

Library of Congress Catalog Card Number: 98-65618

Photo credits:
Cover photo: Carr Clifton © 1998
Noella Ballenger: 12 (left), 20, 27, 31, 41, 43, 65, 76, 79, 87, 88, 112, 115, 126, 129, 130, 138, 143, 154, 161, 162, 168, 182, 203, 208, 210, 215, 225, 228, 234, 250, 255, 269 (left), 279, 289, 290, 292, 307; **Ed Cooper:** 16 (left), 19, 21, 23 (right), 30, 34, 47, 51, 55, 60, 99, 101, 111, 118-119, 132, 147, 152-153, 159, 167, 174, 176, 180, 186-187, 198, 201 (right), 206, 209, 212, 214, 222, 240, 243, 245, 247, 258 (right), 274, 282-283, 285, 300, 302, 311 (right), 318; **Jim Ford:** Title page, 5, 39, 63 (left), 145, 156; **Robert Holmes:** 77, 81, 91, 125, 149, 185; **Dewitt Jones Productions, Inc.:** 44, 67, 69, 122, 148 (bottom), 191, 220, 233 (left), 248-249, 252, 298; **Santokh Kochar:** 16 (right), 54, 140, 173, 236; **Mae Scanlan:** 128, 135, 277, 288, 296 (bottom), 309 (right); **Lee Snider/Photo Images:** 58 (left), 74-75, 82, 84, 114, 171 (top), 216-217, 311 (left), 320; **Tom Stack & Associates:** Tom Algire: 227, 297; D. Holden Bailey: 96; Scott Blackman: 15, 25, 29, 48-49; W. Perry Conway: 272; Gerald A. Corsi: 95; David M. Dennis: 179; Terry Donnelly: 171 (bottom), 269 (right), 284, 309 (left), 315; Ann Duncan: 219; Bill Everitt: 239 (left); Bill & Sally Fletcher: 104; Jeff Foott: 80; Sharon Gerig: 18, 23 (left), 58 (right), 151, 189, 304; John Gerlach: 12 (right), 13, 63 (right), 230, 239 (right); J. Lotter Gurling: 37, 70 (bottom), 193, 233 (right), 265; JPL/TSADO: 105; Thomas Kitchin: 9, 313; Joe McDonald: 6-7; Gary Milburn: 70 (top), 165; NASA/TSADO: 32 (bottom), 194; Mark Newman: 56; Jim Nilsen: 72; Brian Parker: 260; Rod Planck: 204, 235, 258 (left), 267, 275; Bob Pool: 10, 317; Milton Rand: 32 (top), 106, 108; Bob Rozinski: 103; Wendy Shattil: 237; John Shaw: 42, 53, 57, 83, 121, 148 (top), 197, 254, 271, 281, 296 (top); Inga Spence: 116, 262; Tom Stack: 50; Spencer Swanger: 93, 201 (left), 266, 286, 295; William L. Wantland: 244, 319; D. Wilder: 38; **SuperStock:** 256.

Margaret Anne Huffman is an award-wining journalist and former family/lifestyle editor of *The Shelbyville News*. She has also written and contributed to 17 books. Her most recent titles include *A Moment With God for Mothers* and *Through the Valley: Prayers for Violent Times*.

Gary Wilde is a full-time freelance author and editor who has written numerous books, educational materials, and magazine articles on religious and self-help issues. He is the author of *The Bedside Book of Prayer: Devotions for Daily Life* and editor of the devotional quarterly *Quiet Hour*.

Quotations selected by Kacy Gramckow.

Page 19: Excerpt from *Letters to Malcolm: Chiefly on Prayer* by C.S. Lewis, copyright © 1964, 1963 by C.S. Lewis PTE, Ltd. and renewed 1992, 1991 by Arthur Owen Barfield, reprinted by permission of Harcourt Brace & Company. **Page 65:** From *Till Armageddon: A Perspective on Suffering* by Billy Graham, © 1981, Word Publishing, Nashville, Tennessee. All rights reserved. **Page 76:** From *The Collected Verse of Edgar A. Guest* by Edgar A. Guest, © 1984. Used with permission of NTC/Contemporary Publishing Company. **Page 80:** From *Till Armageddon: A Perspective on Suffering* by Billy Graham, © 1981, Word Publishing, Nashville, Tennessee. All rights reserved. **Page 105:** Reprinted from *Anytime Prayers* by Madeleine L'Engle, © 1994 by Crosswicks. Used by permission of Harold Shaw Publishers, Wheaton, IL 60189. **Page 127:** From *Another Day* by Eugenia Price. Copyright © 1984 by Eugenia Price. Used by permission of Doubleday, a division of Bantam Doubleday Dell Publishing Group, Inc. **Page 160:** From *Till Armageddon: A Perspective on Suffering* by Billy Graham, © 1981, Word Publishing, Nashville, Tennessee. All rights reserved. **Page 199:** From *Answers to Life's Problems* by Billy Graham, © 1960, 1988, Word Publishing, Nashville, Tennessee. All rights reserved. **Page 202:** From *Mother Teresa: A Simple Path* compiled by Lucinda Vardey; published by Rider. **Page 236:** Excerpt from *The Sign of Jonas* by Thomas Merton, copyright 1953 by The Abbey of Our Lady of Gethsemani and renewed 1981 by the Trustees of the Merton Legacy Trust, reprinted by permission of Harcourt Brace & Company. **Page 257:** Excerpt from *Carver of Tuskegee* by George Washington Carver used by permission of the Carver Memorial, Diamond, MO. **Page 289:** Taken from *15 Minutes Alone with God* by Emilie Barnes, copyright © 1994 by Harvest House Publishers, Eugene, Oregon. Used by permission. **Page 294:** From *The Root of the Righteous* by A.W. Tozer. Copyright © 1955, 1986 by Lowell Tozer. Reprinted by permission of Christian Publications, Inc. **Page 308:** From *Answers to Life's Problems* by Billy Graham, © 1960, 1988, Word Publishing, Nashville, Tennessee. All rights reserved.

CONTENTS

Talking to God

One, as the song goes, is the loneliest number. Yet throughout our busy, schedule-driven days, that is how we live: trying to go it alone. How silly we are, for there is no need. Through prayer, we become connected to a companion God who is the first to celebrate our joys, the first to cry at our troubles.

Prayer builds a bridge that spans the distance from isolation to awareness of God's presence and availability. Prayer is listening . . . on God's part and ours. A bottomless well from which we can draw, prayer offers strength and light for times of doubt; clarity and guidance during moments of confusion; security for in-between times of change and upheaval; and energy for rebuilding after loss.

Simple Prayers and Blessings is designed to help you know God through word and image. Brief, conversational prayers in everyday language for all circumstances bring you into companionship with a sturdy, ever-present God. The message in each blessing and prayer is simple: We are not alone. Readers are invited into places where this interested and approachable God may be found: wherever we are. For there is no situation that is beyond God's interest and desire for us to use prayer as a resource in responding to it. There is nothing about us that is too ordinary, trivial, or troubling for God to help us redeem it from something useless to something useful.

Reading between the lines of the following pages, we find that wherever we are—shopping, cooking, walking the dog, commuting, watching news, keeping vigil at a hospital bedside, negotiating big business deals, singing "Happy Birthday," paying bills, kneeling at a grave, or holding a newborn—God is there first, waiting for us simply to reach out a hand, listen, and look to discover a caring presence.

We learn in these prayers, expressed in a full range of feelings, that God is sturdy enough to take our doubts and angers and as eager as we to celebrate the good times. By talking with God, we discover a creativity within us that inspires enlightening new ideas, new ventures, new perspectives for looking at old problems. Above all, through prayer, we can live a vigorous hope in the knowledge that nothing can separate us from God's love.

The chapters are landmarks of daily life, finding us at home with our families, at work, in times of celebration and times of trouble, learning life lessons, seeking renewal and healing, in times of transition, and at moments of spiritual insight. The prayers and blessings within each chapter—whether asking, confessing, wondering, seeking, challenging and doubting, or thanking—are starting places for continued nourishment of mind and spirit.

Sometimes the only prayers we have to offer are our fears and angers; at other times, we can only be childlike and hasty. But always, we are assured of God's attention. In the light of this truth, reading and pondering these prayers becomes like planting seeds. They are gifts for us to tend and harvest far beyond the last page.

Beautiful artwork and illustrations offer further illumination, as do uplifting thoughts from scripture and other writings. As you read, it is our hope that you will be reminded of the joy and security that comes from companionship with a God who welcomes our major and minor joys and concerns, our laughter and tears.

Margaret Anne Huffman

CHAPTER ONE

In Times of Celebration

You will go out in joy and be led forth in peace;

the mountains and hills will burst

into song before you.

Isaiah 55:12 NIV

Our Prayer for Earth

For clean air and pure water; for glorious colors in
sky and tree in first and last bloom, in the
wings of migrating butterfly, goose, and bird.
Lord of all, to you we raise our hymn of grateful praise.

For wildlife sanctuaries, open range, prairies, mountains; for
backyard gardens; for corn stalks and bean stems
growing tall then bending low for harvest.
For your generous gifts that meet human need.
Lord of all, to you we raise our hymn of grateful praise.

Every day and night we marvel at your wondrous care.
Constantly you guide our choices, inviting us to creative living.
All creation reflects your empowering love: rolling countryside,
stark canyons, majestic mountains, delicate wildflowers, and
sturdy roadside blooms. Sunrise and star, warmth and
chill all declare your glory, singing together.
Lord of all, to you we raise our hymn of grateful praise.

For love that gives us soul-satisfying happiness; for families,
friends, and all others around us; for loved ones here and
loved ones beyond; for tender, peaceful thoughts.
Lord of all, to you we raise our hymn of grateful praise.

For letting us know you exist through families and friends
who feed us more than enough food, who give us abundant shelter
and clothing, who cherish your presence and honor your creation.
Lord of all, to you we raise our hymn of grateful praise.

For the pleasure of seeing your wonderful creation; for the pleasure
of hearing other voices and music; for the delight of knowing and feeling;
for gathering us in families and communities; for inspiring us to stretch
toward new knowledge, heightened awareness; for the blending
of all experience into the excitement we call life. Lord of all,
to you we raise our hymn of grateful praise.

Today: Cause for Celebration

*With boldness and wonder and expectation, I greet you this morning,
God of sunrise and rising dew. Gratefully, I look back to all that was
good yesterday and in hope, face forward, ready for today.*

Sing Praise for Today

May you celebrate this day with all your heart.
Rejoice in the beauty of its light and warmth.
Give thanks for the air and grass and sidewalks.
Let gratitude for other faces flow into your soul.
And cherish the chance to work and play, to think and speak—
*   knowing this: All simple pleasures are opportunities for praise.*

In Thanks for a Good Day

How fortunate I feel today!
All is well.
Things are working out.
But is it luck . . . or is it your love?
I will assume the latter
and offer words of praise:
Bless your name, Almighty One!

Were there no God, we would be in this glorious world

with grateful hearts: and no one to thank.

Christina Georgina Rossetti

Blessed Baby, Welcome

*Bless this newborn, Lord, with hunger of soul and mind to match a growing,
thriving body. At awesome moments like these, we, your "big children,"
feel your blessing wrapped around us like a baby's blanket. Give us wisdom,
patience, humor, stamina, humility, joy, and grace to pass on.*

A Beautiful Gift

*How marvelous our bodies!
May we care for them today with all the
reverence and honor we might extend
toward any great gift that defies explanation.*

How Beautiful You Are

Happy birthday to you!
That was a good day, and you were there.
Everyone who saw you thought:
"How beautiful!"
So take a moment in front of the mirror:
Still beautiful, no matter how you look.
For God sees only your loveliness.
From day one.

Blessing for a Newborn

Bless this little one of so few days.
May he be prosperous in all his ways.
Healthy in body and mind,
Growing strong and kind.
Bless this little one through all his days.

Thanksgiving is nothing if not a glad and reverent lifting of the heart to God

in honour and praise for His goodness.

James R. Miller

Milestone Birthday Blessing

Bless this candle-lit festival of birthday celebration, Lord, for our special loved one. Join us as we blow out candles and joke about setting the cake ablaze, about golden ages and silver hairs. Our laughter is bubbling up from gratitude that the years are only enriching this special celebrant. We are grateful that the years are also enriching our *lives as friends and family as well, for we are the ones receiving the best birthday gift today: the gift of knowing this special person. Thank you for sharing.*

Blessed Teens

This birthday, Lord, my child becomes a teen.
Surely it's just the smoke of thirteen candles making me cry.
But, O Lord, wasn't it just yesterday that there was just a single candle?

From before that day to this, I've trusted you. I ask you now to bless the youthful drive to risk making choices; the struggle to be heard; the changing body, moods, and mind. Bless—and this is hardest for me to say—the urge for independence.

Bless me with ears to listen, a shoulder to lean on, and the good sense to build bridges, not walls.

Blessed is the man who does

not walk in the counsel

of the wicked or stand

in the way of sinners or sit

in the seat of mockers.

But his delight is in the law

of the Lord, and on his law

he meditates day and night.

He is like a tree planted

by streams of water, which

yields its fruit in season

and whose leaf does not wither.

Whatever he does prospers.

Psalm 1 NIV

Tapestry of Marriage

From our first shy "I love you" to today's public vow, you pulled us like two strands from the tangled world and brought us together. Each is distinct and colorful but joined now so lovingly that sorrow—and joy likewise—for one will be felt by the other.

A Wedding Prayer

During this wedding, may all who attend find time to reflect on the glory of human relationships—reflections, as they are, of the goodness of God.

Wedding Blessing

Bless the couple before you, Lord, with the best marriage has to share:
*   peace, not of a stagnant pond, but of deep rivers flowing;*
strength, not of sheltered dogwood, but of oak, sycamore, and beech,
*   storm-tossed and rooted;*
power, not of fists and temper, but of seed stretching toward the sun.

Rehearsal Dinner Grace:
A Prayer for Beginnings

Welcome to our party, Lord of water-into-wine feastings.
Stand with us as we honor two special people poised at the edge
of a great venture. Be with them on this, the final eve of their
separateness, for soon they will become a union.
Be present at their daily table as you are with them around
this festive banquet now. Be with us, too, their friends and family,
as we share a meal, a memory, and a toast for new beginnings.

The path of the righteous is like the first gleam of dawn,

shining ever brighter till the full light of day.

Proverbs 4:18 NIV

A Palm Sunday Grace

We gather this day around a table of celebration, shouting welcome and
"Hosanna!" Yet, as children do in play when given palm fronds as
tokens of remembrance, we so quickly turn them into swords.
Take away our love of violence, our way of creating weapons from
peaceable moments. And for us at this table, God of lions and lambs,
heal any hurt feelings, saddened hearts, and lonely days so that we
can truly celebrate being together this day in a crowd of friends and family.
We have a long week ahead before we celebrate again.

Small Miracles

Bless you, Lord!
The heavens declare your glory;
the skies proclaim your mighty power.
And here I am, looking up into
those vast regions, knowing
that the tiniest cell in my body
is a most glorious miracle, as well.
Bless you, Lord!

We—or at least I—shall not be able to adore God on the highest

occasions if we have learned no habit of doing so on the lowest.

At best, our faith and reason will tell us that He is adorable,

but we shall not have found Him so, not have "tasted and seen."

Any patch of sunlight in a wood will show you something about

the sun which you could never get from reading books on astronomy.

These pure and spontaneous pleasures are "patches of Godlight"

in the woods of our experience.

C. S. Lewis, *The Quotable Lewis: Letters to Malcom: Chiefly on Prayer*

Blessings on the Anniversary Couple

There is no greater mystery than love, Lord of covenants and promises. We are in its presence on this anniversary day. Bless those who live, day after day after ordinary day, within the fullness of married love, surely one of the greatest mysteries. Bless them as they honor their past, even while they create a future. Let them bask in the pleasures and applause of today, when we bow before their accomplishments which, like the rings we read on the inner souls of trees, are an inspiration and blessing to us all.

See! The winter is past;

 the rains are over and gone.

Flowers appear on the earth;

 the season of singing has come,

the cooing of doves

 is heard in our land.

The fig tree forms its early fruit;

 the blossoming vines spread their fragrance.

Arise, come, my darling,

 my beautiful one, come with me.

Song of Solomon 2:11–13 NIV

Happy Anniversary

*Thank you, Lord, for our marriage. Like a wedding band,
our love encircles but doesn't bind. Like a vow, our love is words
but sustains because of what they mean. In your grace, our love
has the permanence of rock, not of walls, but of a bridge to moments
ahead as special and bright as when we first met.*

In Praise of the Usual

So much to celebrate, Lord: waking to dawn gilding trees;
squeezing fresh orange juice, its zest clinging to my hands all day;
making a new friend, talking to an old one; watching the first leaf bud,
raking the last. Each day's turning brings gifts from you to celebrate.

I Did It!

O Lord, I savor this triumph: I met my goal!
Day by day, I reached into my heart and found energy to keep on.
Day by day, I reached out and found your hand leading, your inspiration
guiding. Stand with me to accept applause for our joint success.

In Good Times

Bless us in this time of good fortune.
Give us the grace to be grateful for newfound comforts,
magnanimous among those who have less, and
thoroughly giving with all we've been given. Amen.

Of all good gifts that the Lord lets fall,
Is not silence the best of all?

The deep, sweet hush when the song is closed,
And every sound but a voiceless ghost;

And every sigh, as we listening leant,
A breathless quiet of vast content?

The laughs we laughed have a purer ring
With but their memory echoing;

So of all good gifts that the Lord lets fall,
Is not silence the best of all?

James Whitcomb Riley, "Best of All"

Love is patient, love is kind. It does not envy, it does not boast, it is not proud.

It is not rude, it is not self-seeking, it is not easily angered, it keeps no record of wrongs.

Love does not delight in evil but rejoices with the truth.

It always protects, always trusts, always hopes, always perseveres.

Love never fails. But where there are prophecies, they will cease;

where there are tongues, they will cease; where there is knowledge, it will pass away.

For we know in part and we prophesy in part, but when perfection comes,

the imperfect disappears. When I was a child, I talked like a child,

I thought like a child, I reasoned like a child.

When I became a man, I put childish ways behind me.

Now we see but a poor reflection as in a mirror; then we shall see face to face.

Now I know in part; then I shall know fully, even as I am fully known.

And now these three remain: faith, hope and love. But the greatest of these is love.

1 Corinthians 13:4–13 NIV

Blessings for Grandparents on Their Day

They've added a new holiday, Lord, a day to honor the grandparents
who tended us so well. Pause with us as we play again in the dusty lanes of childhood
at Grandma and Grandpa's house. Bless these bigger-than-life companions who helped
us bridge home and away, childhood and maturity. In their footsteps, we made
the journey. Thank you for such a heritage and a day on which to express our gratitude.

First Day of Advent

*Connected in memory to holidays past, like links in a colorful
paper chain decorating the tree, we begin another advent.
Some recollections are happy and pleasant, others sad and empty, yet each
brings us to this new starting point, as fresh and full of promise as an egg
about to hatch. Make all things new this holiday, even old
memories, for this is the season of second chances.*

Grace for Advent

*You are a welcome guest at this table, God, as we pause
in the midst of this bell-ringing, carol-making
season of too much to do.
Send us your gift of silent nights so that we can hear and
know what you will be bringing us this year: yet another gift of hope.
Bless our gathering around this table; we will set a
place each day for you.
Join us in our daily feast, for which we now give thanks.
May it nourish our busy bodies as the
anticipation of your presence among us
does our weary spirits.*

Celebrate the Word!

May you rejoice in the written Word.
The scriptures can come alive for you;
only take, and read.
Discover the acts of God in history.
Travel with his disciples along
the pathway of service.
See how his church began,
how it grew
down through the centuries.
Yes, celebrate the written Word,
for it is a mirror of,
and a witness to, the Living
Word of the heavens.

Getting Ready for Christmas

*We are such stubborn folk, gentle God, only moving toward you when it's
time for a baby, of all things! What an illogical story, yet you knew it
would take something unexpected to get our attention.
Be with us as we edge toward the manger again this year, both from
curiosity and habit, pausing to kneel there because we are
finally getting the message.*

A Small Prayer While Wrapping Presents

*Tangled in tape, lists, and holiday wrappings, we are all thumbs of excitement!
Bless the surprises we've selected, wrapped, and hidden.
Restore us to the joy of anticipation. We want to be surprised, too.
Our wish lists include the gift of peace possibilities, of ears to
hear a summons and eyes to spot another's need or
triumph, of being able to make a difference.*

*As we cut and tape, God of surprises, remind us to keep in
touch with the gift's recipient after the wrapping papers are
long gone and the ornaments packed.*

28

'Twas the Night Before Christ: A Christmas Eve Grace

The Christmas tree, O God, is groaning beneath gift-wrapped anticipation. The table spead before us is resplendent with shared foods prepared by loving hands, for which we give thanks.

And now, as this waiting season ticks to a bell-ringing, midnight-marvelous close, we around this table are scooting over to make room for the anticipated Guest. Come, blessing us with the gift of your presence as we say, "Welcome."

A Celebration of Giving

Be ready to offer your gentle touch today—and celebrate the gift of kindness.
Reach out to the elderly and infirm. Stretch out your hand to the children and infants.
Do not hold back.
Celebrate by letting your warmth flow through.
And rejoice in your ability to do God's will in this way.

Blessing for a New Year

The slate is clean, Lord, the calendar as bare as the Christmas tree.
Bless the New Year that beckons. We sing of you as help in ages past but need
to know you as hope for years to come. Help us face what we must,
celebrate every triumph we can, and make changes we need.
We're celebrating to the fullest this whistle-blowing, toast-raising moment,
for it is the threshold between the old and the new us.

Forgiven

Celebrate!
I am forgiven!
The conflict is over.
The animosity long forgotten.
How wonderful to be set free from rancor.
How good to have a friend instead of an enemy.
How beautiful our renewed friendship.
I am forgiven!
Celebrate!

Thou, my all! My theme!

My inspiration! and my crown!

My strength in age—my rise in low estate!

My soul's ambition, pleasure,

wealth!—my world! My light in darkness!

and my life in death!

My boast through time! bliss through eternity! Eternity, too

short to speak thy praise!

Or fathom thy profound love to man!

Edward Young, *Night Thoughts,* "Night IV"

A Blessing of Love

May the blessing of God fill your days. Especially, may you develop the perfect balance of duties to family and responsibilities at work and worship. As you seek serenity in these things, may you find great cause for celebration, knowing that the one who loves you unconditionally remains at the center of all your activity.

Celebrate Love

May you enjoy all the streams of love that flow into your life:
The love from family and friends;
The love from parents and children;
The love from pets
*   and the love from God.*
Celebrate love all day long.
For it is the breath of your existence,
*   and the best of all reasons for living.*

The Summer Fruits now gathered in,

Let thankful Hearts in chearful

Looks be seen;

Ope the hospitable Gate,

Ope for Friendship, not for State;

Neighbours and Strangers enter there

Equal to all of honest Air;

To Rich or Poor of Soul sincere.

Cheap bought Plenty, artless Store,

Feed the Rich, and fill the Poor;

Converse chear the sprightly Guest,

Cordial Welcome crown the Feast;

Easy Wit with Candour fraught,

Laughter genuine and unsought;

Jest from double Meaning free,

Blameless harmless Jollity;

Mirth, that no repenting Gloom

Treasures for our Years to come.

Ben Franklin, *Poor Richard's Almanack*

34

A Blessing for Memorial Day: The Gift of History

Surrounded by a community of headstones, we remember and mourn, celebrate and play, God of history and future. We place our bouquets on overgrown graves and our picnic lunches on family reunion tables. And we feel grateful for our history written by strangers fallen in battle to insure our freedom-filled lives of safety. Our ancestors' efforts are remembered throughout our lives in strengths, names, and accomplishments that we now pause and honor.

Bless our picnics and parties as we join in the parade of those remembering, those remembered.

True Vision

I see it clearly now:
Everything that has happened first passed though
the office of heaven and was stamped: Approved!
Therefore I will rejoice instead of complaining.
I will celebrate instead of railing against your will.
If these events have a purpose, I will seek it out.
If there is a reason, I will try to find it.
I see it clearly now.

An Easter Meal Grace

*We are celebrating today, O God, a mixture of bunnies hiding
colored eggs and angels rolling away stones. Join us as we
gather to share a meal and ponder both,
enjoying the one and giving thanks for the other.
Bless those at this table savoring the food and the message of this day.
Remind us, too, Lord of unexpected appearances, that this
also is the season of spring, a time when rebirth is not so
surprising after all. Send us after lunch into the yard where,
hiding colored Easter eggs for the children, we may
understand anew what this day really means.*

Grace for Our Feast

*We gather around this feasting table, humbled by our bounty,
Lord of abundant life; we have so much more than we need.
We confess that we are poised, fork in hand, ready to overdo.
Help us learn better how to live as grateful, if overstuffed,
children—delighted, surprised, and generous with the
sharing of our good fortune. Bless us now as we enjoy it
amidst food, friends, and family. We give the heartiest
thanks for your diligent, steadfast care.*

Caught up in Traditions

We're caught up in well-worn, comfy traditions, Lord. Keep them worthy,
for like a deer path through the forest, they lead us forward and back.
Thank you for the divine love and holiness found in the ordinary.

For all the Saints:
A Prayer for Halloween

Amidst hobgoblins and pranksters,
O God, we seek a quiet corner this autumn
evening to give thanks for the saints
whose day this really is.
Be tolerant of our commercialized,
costumed hoopla, even as you
remind us of the pillars upon
which our faith rests today.
Keep our trick-or-treating fun,
clean, and safe and our
faith memories aware, for it is too
easy to lose track of what we
really celebrate in the
darkness of this night.

Not Alone

Go in peace. You are not alone in the world. Rejoice in friendships, fellowships, acquaintances, parties, and get-togethers of every kind. You are not alone. Rejoice.

Graduation Day

*Skipping up the sidewalk . . . first day of school. Reading, writing, 'rithmetic.
Frst steps, first dates, first jobs. Hurrying down the sidewalk,
diploma in hand . . . last day of school.*

*What more can I say, dear God, than I've said since before my beloved
graduate was born? Watch over and visit this young person with your presence.
We've done a pretty good job so far, you and I.
And now it's time to let go. Be with me.
I'm better at roots than wings. Remind me that
nothing can separate us from one another or your love.*

*Help me be there for my children as you are for me,
companion God. Go with this child today. I mustn't follow too
closely, and I can't yet judge my distance.*

O perfect Love, all human thought transcending, Lowly we kneel in prayer before thy throne,

That theirs may be the love which knows no ending, Whom Thou for evermore dost join in one.

O perfect Life, Be Thou their full assurance Of tender charity and steadfast faith,

Of patient hope, and quiet, brave endurance, with childlike trust that fears nor pain nor death.

Grant them the joy which brightens earthly sorrow,

Grant them the peace which calms all earthly strife, And to life's day

the glorious unknown morrow that dawns upon eternal love and life.

Dorothy Gurney, *O Perfect Love*

A New Beginning

What a blessing to have a second chance!
Grant me the wisdom to use this opportunity wisely.
And save me from the fear that I'll fall into the same old traps as last time.
This is a brand new day, a whole new beginning. Fanstastic!

For One Who Lives Well

Blessed are you who know how to celebrate the goodness of life.
Blessed because you choose to see the grace above and beyond the pain.
Blessed because you see a potential friend in every stranger you meet.
Blessed because you know the darkest clouds have brilliant silver linings.
And most blessed because:
  All you ever knew of the half-empty glass was that it was almost full.

On the Blessings of Life

Go forth in the joy of the Lord,
  knowing how blessed you are.
Celebrate the beauty of nature around you.
Celebrate the goodness of fellowship with others.
Celebrate the opportunity to grow and learn
  and take up the challenge of each new day.
Most of all: celebrate your life.
  How blessed you are!

43

44

Thanks-living

Some prayers are best left unfinished, God of abundance,
and this will be an ongoing conversation between us.
Each day, I discover new gifts you offer me, and the list of reasons
to be thankful grows.

As I accept your gifts and live with them thankfully, guide me to become a
person who shares with others so that they, too,
can live abundantly. May someone, somewhere, someday
say of me, "I am thankful to have this person in my life."

A Sense of Wonder

In this beautiful place, there are wonders all around me, God, I know.
The only thing lacking is wonder. Lift up my heart in praise!

Together

Bless this partnership, God, the friendship of her and me.
And remind us both: Every gathering of two
is really a fellowship of three.

When I had made speech my own, I could not wait to go home.

At last the happiest of happy moments arrived.

I had made my homeward journey, talking constantly to

Miss Sullivan, not for the sake of talking,

but determined to improve to the last minute.

Almost before I knew it, the train stopped at the

Tuscumbia station, and there on the platform

stood the whole family. My eyes fill with tears now as I

think how my mother pressed me close to her,

speechless and trembling with delight,

taking in every syllable that I spoke, while little

Mildred seized my free hand and kissed it and danced,

and my father expressed his pride and affection in a big silence.

It was as if Isaiah's prophecy had been fulfilled in me,

"The mountains and hills shall break forth before you into singing, and

all the trees of the field shall clap their hands!"

Helen Keller, *The Story of My Life*

He Is There

Know the benediction of the Lord in these days!
In all your comings and goings, know he is there. In all your joys and triumphs,
know he upholds you. In all your worries and heartaches, know that he cares.
And in all your worship, celebrating, dancing, laughing—wherever
you are—know that he is pleased.

CHAPTER TWO

In Times of Trouble

I would rather walk with God

in the dark than go

alone in the light.

Mary Gardiner Brainard, *Not Knowing*

Always With Us

We know there is no greater burden than to think no one cares or understands.
That is why the promise of your presence is so precious to us, you who said:
"Remember, I am with you always, to the end of the age."

Lighten our darkness, Lord, we pray; and in your mercy defend us from all

perils and dangers of this night; for the love of your only Son, our Saviour Jesus Christ. Amen.

Gelasian Sacramentary, "An Evening Prayer"

Prayer for Between Jobs

The layoff is ice in the mind.
Who am I now? What can I do?
This is all I've done. The questions range the pay scale,
for being laid off, Lord, is an equal opportunity ambush.
As we wait to be called back, inspire us to make
our job that of hunting another job. Somewhere we'll
be needed again. Stand with us in the waiting lines.

The Barriers Inside

Lord, I wish to live a long life,
   but I fear growing old.
I want to accomplish great things,
   but I fear risking what I already have.
I desire to love with all my heart,
   but the prospect of self-revelation makes me shrink back.
Perhaps for just this day,
   you would help me reach out?
Let me bypass these dreads and see instead
   your hand reaching back to mine—
   right now—just as it always has.

51

Sticks and Stones

No matter how hard I try, God of patience and support, someone finds fault with me. I am mortified about the latest criticism. I can't decide whether to run away in shame or storm back and defend my actions, for I thought I was right.

Criticism hurts most when coupled with ridicule, and I feel like less of a person for the tone in which I was addressed. Give me the courage to confront this, Lord, for it is not acceptable to be treated this way even when in error. Keep me calm, factual, and open; perhaps the tone was unintentional, the critic unaware of the power of shaming.

Help me remember how I feel now the next time I find fault with someone. As I've learned firsthand with you the zillions of times I messed up, there are better ways to confront mistakes than with stinging criticisms that divide and demean. Truth be known, Lord, such abrasive manners say more about the criticizer than the criticized. Keep me from passing them on.

Room for One More

Opposites don't attract nearly as often as they repel, if we are to believe the headlines. Pick a race, color, creed, or lifestyle, Lord of all, and we'll find something to fight about. Deliver us from stereotypes. Inspire us to spot value in everyone we meet. As we dodge the curses and hatred, we are relieved there is room for all beneath your wings. Bless our diversity; may it flourish.

So Little Time

Square by square, we live our lives marked off in neat appointment-calendar blocks of time. Everybody gets only so much, no more, for the lines are already bulging. We pencil in commitments that spill over into tomorrow's squares. And just look at yesterday's notations: Nowhere did we get every "to do" done, every deadline met.

There is not enough time in the little squares we have allotted ourselves, O God, calling them life. We try using a larger calendar with bigger squares, but all we do is schedule heavier. Our pencils eat up our best intentions for accepting your promised abundant life.

Help us, for we want to be more than just the sum of all we had scheduled, minus what we got done, multiplied by what we wished we'd been doing, tallying up to a bottom line of regret.

Guide us as we erase what is not essential. Forgive us for the day-squares where we've inched you out; their hectic dreariness reflects your absence.

I believe sympathy is one of the most helpful helps one can bestow upon one's fellow creatures; and it seems a great pity that so many people feel it is their duty to criticize rather than sympathize.

Hannah Whitall Smith

Seeking Courage

Seeking courage, Lord,
*   I bundle my fears*
*   and place them in your hands.*
Too heavy for me,
*   too weighty even to ponder*
*   in this moment,*
such shadowy terrors shrink
*   to size in my mind*
*   and—how wonderful!—*
wither to nothing in your grasp.

Man of Sorrows

Man of Sorrows, see my grieving
heart this day. Keep me from
feelings of shame, though,
as I let the loss wash over me.
For this is a part of my life too,
the life only you could give me:
to learn what it means to let go.

55

Rainbow of Confession

We're stained, like a paint rag, by troubles we caused ourselves, Lord. Red, the color of lost temper and rudeness. Green, envy of others who have it easier and more of it. Blue, the shade of despair over something we could change. Yellow, of cowardly running.

Rearrange our unsightly smudges into glorious rainbows through your gift of forgiveness.

Amazing grace!
How sweet the sound
That saved a wretch like me;
I once was lost, but now I'm found;
Was blind, but now I see.
'Twas grace that taught my heart to fear,
And grace my fears relieved;
How precious did that grace appear
The hour I first believed.
Through many dangers, toils and snares
I have already come,
'Tis grace that brought me safe thus far,
And grace will lead me home.

John Newton, "Amazing Grace"

Lovable Differences

Bless our differences, O Lord.
And let us love across all barriers,
*   the walls we build of color,*
*   and culture, and language.*
Let us turn our eyes upward and remember:
The God who made us all lives
*   and breathes and moves within us,*
*   untouched by our petty distinctions.*
Let us love him as he is,
*   for he loves us just as we are.*

In thankfulness for present mercies, nothing so becomes us as losing sight of past ills.

Lew Wallace, *Ben Hur*

Peaks and Valleys

A chart of my efforts to change traces a jagged course, Lord,
like the lines on a heart-rate monitor. Reassure me that instead
of measuring my failures, ups and downs mean simply that
I am alive and ever-changing. Help me become consistent but,
O God, deliver me from flat lines.

The Whole Package

Dear God, complaints sometimes come first before I can feel free to love you. Sometimes you seem distant and unreasonable, uncaring. Help me understand why life can be so hurtful and hard. Hear my complaints and, in the spirit of compassion, show me how to move through pain to rebirth.

Is It Me?

Why can't we seem to get along, Lord? Is it me? For a few moments, I will just be silent . . . to listen for your answer.

A Blessing for Failure

*Bless my attempts at success, Lord, though I know many of them will end in failure.
I pray that you will even bless my failures, for I also know that never risking
is a sure sign of sloth and a questioning of your constant goodwill toward me.*

When in Doubt

*Life has made the most hopeful among us skeptical, Lord of truth. Much is bogus,
and we are uncertain. Thank you for the gift of doubt, for it sparks our seeking.
Keep us lively and excited as we set off on quests blessed by you,
heeding your advice to* knock, seek, ask.

God is our refuge and strength,

> an ever-present help in trouble.

Therefore we will not fear, though the earth give way

> and the mountains fall into the heart of the sea,

though its waters roar and foam

> and the mountains quake with their surging.

The Lord Almighty is with us.

Psalm 46:1–3, 7 NIV

Have mercy on me,

O God, have mercy on me,

for in you my soul takes refuge.

I will take refuge in the shadow of

your wings until the disaster has passed.

I cry out to God Most High, to God,

who fulfills his purpose for me.

He sends from heaven and saves me,

rebuking those who hotly pursue me:

God sends his love and his faithfulness.

Psalm 57:1–3 NIV

Perspective

Abide in peace, knowing that this is not the first time such trouble has entered the human race. And it is not the kind of crisis that makes a difference to life and death. It will not shed blood or cause great suffering.

Yes, it is a problem—with the one, primary quality that characterizes all such tribulations: They all, eventually, come to an end.

Revenge

We know that revenge will settle nothing at this point.
It will only leave us with an emptier feeling than before.
Heal the pain in our hurts over this injustice,
and somehow, as impossible as it now seems, bring us to the place
of blessing our enemies and extending the one thing that keeps
saving our own lives: your forgiveness.

Unfair

Life's not fair, and I stomp my foot in frustration.
The powerful get more so as the rest of us shrink, dreams for peace are shattered
as bullies get the upper hand, and despair is as tempting as an ice cream sundae.
Help me hold on, for you are a God of justice and dreams, of turning life
upside down. Let me help; thanks for listening in the meantime.

Strangers at the Door

How can we recognize any of your needful ones we are to feed,
clothe, and tend, Lord, when we see menace in every outstretched hand?
Inspire and help us reclaim our world for living in, not hiding from.

My Mother Died

I don't belong to anyone now, Lord. My mother died today.
Who will recall the stories of my birth? My first loose tooth? First day of school?
Who will tell me I'm special, perfect, and always welcome no matter what?

Reach out to me, a little child again, lost and frightened and suddenly orphaned.
I'm no more than a marionette holding my own strings, no one on the other end.
Stay with me until I fall asleep and be here should I awake, frightened.
Let me be a child tonight. Tomorrow I'll be strong as befitting the new
matriarch of this family. But for now, Lord, find me, hold me.

Although today He prunes my twigs with pain,

Yet doth His blood nourish and warm my root:

Tomorrow I shall put forth buds again

And clothe myself with fruit.

Christina Georgina Rossetti, "From House to House"

God pardons like a mother who kisses the offense into everlasting forgetfulness.

Henry Ward Beecher

Apart

Bless us both in this time of separation.
May we use the time wisely
to consider our shortcomings,
to seek ways to amend our faults,
and to reconnect the relationship
with a deeper love.

63

Divorce

I never meant to be a failure, O God of covenants and promises.
I never meant to break vows solemnly made. But I am and I did. Comfort me as I
mourn the truth that I could not be okay and remain in that marriage.

Comfort me as I leave behind the familiar—friends, surroundings,
assumptions, home, and connections. I also lose all of them in this "settlement."
Lead me toward other friends and new landmarks, but let this
new life not be created quickly and casually,
Lord, as if divorce is no more serious than clipping one's fingernails.
Enable me to learn something from this grieving passage so that my
mistakes don't get repeated and I roll out of one non-okay
marriage into another without missing a beat.

Be with me now, Lord, as I leave not only a familiar place, but a familiar me.
Grant me wisdom to go forward now, toward a new home and life, solitary but free.
Be with me; the way home has never seemed longer.

In Danger Species

These are mean-spirited times, and we quake and shudder.
Tend us, loving Creator, and shelter us in the palm of your hand against all
that would uproot and destroy us. We are the flowers of your field.

Comfort and prosperity have never enriched the world as adversity has done.

Out of pain and problems have come the sweetest songs, the most poignant poems,

the most gripping stories. Out of suffering and tears have come

the greatest spirits and most blessed lives.

Billy Graham, *Till Armageddon*

All One

You have said: We are all one.
So when I am tempted to separate, alienate,
exasperate my sisters and brothers, remind me: We are all one.

Cups Running Over with Anger

What, God of peace, are we to do with our anger? In the wake of trouble, it fills us to overflowing. Sometimes our anger is the only prayer we can bring you. We are relieved and grateful to know that you are sturdy enough to bear all we feel and say.

Where do we go from here? Is there life after fury?
What will we be without our anger when it's all that has fueled us?

When we are still, we hear your answer: "Emptied."

But then we would be nothing.

Remind us that, in your redeeming hands, nothing *can become of great use, as a gourd hollowed out becomes a cup or a bowl only when emptied.*

When the time comes for us to empty ourselves of this abundance of anger, make us into something useful. It would be a double tragedy to waste anger's re-creative energy.

Hate Hurts

Somebody hates me and is trying to get others to hate me, too. How quickly bad news travels. Okay, Lord, I'll just hate back. I don't want to pray for this hateful person, even as I admit life must be rough to make them so mean-spirited.

Hey, but does that make hating okay?

Help me balance compassion for haters with accountability. This prayer has no end, for I need to work through this. Help me and soon, for there are real wounds in your world to heal, not just my hurt feelings.

Healing Failure

I blew it. Give me courage to admit my mistake, apologize, and go on. Keep me from getting stuck in denial, despair, and, worst of all, fear of trying again. In your remolding hands, God of grace, failures can become feedback and mistakes can simply be lessons in what doesn't work. Remind me that perfection means "suited to the task," not "without mistakes." There's a world of difference.

For Everyone in Times of Trouble

O Lord, hear my prayer for all who are in trouble this day.
Comfort those who are:

> *facing the loss of a loved one. After the wrenching grief,*
> *let their lonely hours be filled with fond memories of days gone by;*
> *passing their days without work. During this time of financial stress,*
> *give them energy to make their employment the job of finding new work.*

Encourage those who are:

> *finding it difficult to believe in the future. Let your hope*
> *fill their hearts as they recall all your past faithfulness;*
> *doubting the truth of your existence or the validity of your promises.*
> *Bring wise friends into their lives who have long known the reality of your love;*
> *struggling to make ends meet. Let them be assured that you can take care*
> *of every need, no matter how large or small.*

Heal those who are:

> *suffering pain and illness. Let them find rest and calm as they seek*
> *to make the idle moments pass more quickly;*
> *racked in mind and stressed out emotionally.*
> *Cradle their minds in your love and soothe every*
> *irrational thought that seeks to run out of control.*

Uphold those who are:
being tempted in any way today. Especially those who may want to end their lives.
Show them that while there is life there is hope, that change is the only constant,
and that change for the better is so likely;
looking at all the negative aspects of life and finding it depressing.
May they find joy in just one moment at a time.
And may that be enough for now.

In all these ways I ask your blessing upon those in trouble.
And please include me in that blessing, too!

69

He Is There

*May you be assured of God's
presence as you weather this storm.
As the waves toss you about,
and the ship of your life
threatens to crash into rough rocks:
He is there. Never despair.
For no wind or water,
rock or sand has the power to
defeat his plans for you.
And, after all, he created all
these things, and in him alone
they have their existence.*

Blessed are the poor in spirit,

   for theirs is the kingdom of heaven.

Blessed are those who mourn, for they will be comforted.

Blessed are the meek, for they will inherit the earth.

Blessed are those who hunger and thirst for righteousness,

   for they will be filled.

Blessed are the merciful, for they will be shown mercy.

Blessed are the pure in heart, for they will see God.

Blessed are the peacemakers, for they

   will be called sons of God.

Blessed are those who are persecuted because

   of righteousness, for theirs is the kingdom of heaven.

Blessed are you when people insult you, persecute you

   and falsely say all kinds of evil against you because of me.

   Rejoice and be glad, because great is your reward in heaven.

Matthew 5:3–12 NIV

When you have no helpers, see all your helpers in God.

When you have many helpers, see God in all your helpers.

When you have nothing but God, see all in God; when you have everything,

see God in everything. Under all conditions, stay thy heart only on the Lord.

Charles Haddon Spurgeon

Minding Our Manners

It's hard to be pleasant these rude, road-raging days.

Everyone's too immersed in their own concerns to be mannerly or kind.

Encourage me to get in the first words of "please," "thanks," and "excuse me";

nudge me to be first to take turns on the road, in the store, at work.

Maybe good manners will be as catching as rude ones; may I,

with your guidance, be first to pass them on.

You can talk to God because God listens.

Your voice matters in heaven. He takes you very seriously.

When you enter his presence, the attendants turn to you to hear your voice.

No need to fear that you will be ignored. Even if you stammer or stumble,

even if what you have to say impresses no one,

it impresses God—and he listens.

He listens to the painful plea of the elderly in the rest home.

He listens to the gruff confession of the death-row inmate.

When the alcoholic begs for mercy, when the spouse seeks guidance,

when the businessman steps off the street into the chapel, God listens.

Max Lucado, *The Great House of God, A Home for Your Heart*

CHAPTER THREE

At Home

Prayer is needed for children and in families.

Love begins at home and that is why it is important to pray

together. If you pray together you will stay together and

love each other as God loves each one of you.

Mother Teresa of Calcutta, *A Simple Path*

For all the beauties of the day,
The innocence of childhood's play,
For health and strength and laughter sweet,
Dear Lord, our thanks we now repeat.

For this our daily gift of food
We offer now our gratitude,
For all the blessings we have known
Or debt of gratefulness we own.

Here at the table now we pray,
Keep us together down the way;
May this, our family circle, be
Held fast by love and unity.

Grant, when the shades of night shall fall,
Sweet be the dreams of one and all;
And when another day shall break
Unto Thy service may we wake.

Edgar A. Guest, *Grace at Evening*

The Faces of Love

*Bless my family, Lord. They are a gift from you, evidence of your unwillingness
    for me to be alone. Until I see you face to face, may the faces
    of those I love be to me as your own.*

Peace in Our Home

*Let your peace rest upon our home, dear God.
We do not know how to love one another as you have loved us.
We fail to reach out the way you have gathered us in.
We forget how to give when only taking fills our minds.
And, most of all, we need your presence to know
we are more than just parents and children.
We are always your beloved sons and daughters here.
Let your peace rest upon our home, dear God.*

Love-Built Home

*Bless all that happens here, O God, planner and builder. May we find laughter and love
and strength and sanctuary. Bless all who visit our love-built home, family and
companions with whom we can grow. May we, like you, offer shelter and welcome.*

Home, Blessed Home

Home. The word rolls on the tongue like bubble gum,
soft and sweet and reminiscent
Where better to think of you, Lord, than at home?
It is where we have our history, begin our traditions, take our rites of passage.
It is where we are first loved, first safe, first found to be special.
It is where we are sheltered and nourished, then equipped and sent on our way.

Throughout it all, you sit invisibly in our midst, yet are central,
blessing our kitchens, where we receive and provide nourishment; bedrooms, giving us
restorative sleep; yards and gardens, connecting us with your creation;
windows and doors, letting in light and air; basements and attics,
sustaining us in ways we often overlook; living rooms, arranging us in
"come as you are" circles of families and friends.

We feel your blessing on our lived-in homes. Help us see the beauty,
the opportunities in them. Bless us, the homebodies.

Peace Be With You

This is my benediction upon you: that peace be with you all the days of your life,
and that you dwell in the house of the Lord forever.

Sanctuary

Source of all life and love, let this family be
a place of warmth on a cold night,
a friendly haven for the lonely stranger,
a small sanctuary of peace in the midst of swirling activity.
Above all, let all its members seek to reflect the kindness
of your own heart, day by day.

These Blessings, Reader,
    may Heav'n grant to thee;

A faithful Friend, equal in Love's degree;

Land fruitful, never conscious of the Curse,

A liberal Heart and never-failing Purse;

A smiling Conscience, a contented mind;

A temp'rate Knowledge with true

    Wisdom join'd;

A Life as long as fair, and when expir'd,

A kindly Death, unfear'd as undesire'd.

Ben Franklin, *Poor Richard's Almanack*

Almost everyone likes to beautify his home. There is something lacking in a home where there are no flowers, no pictures on the walls, where no effort at all has been put forth to make the home attractive.

Few of us here have homes as beautiful as we would like, but everyone in heaven will find it beautiful beyond imagination. Heaven could not help but be so, because it is the Father's house and He is a God of beauty.

Look at the world around us. God made it! Whether we live amid the snow and ice of Alaska or under the palm trees of California or Florida, we have beauty.

Billy Graham, *Till Armageddon*

A Roof Over Our Heads

Bless this roof over our heads, and keep it from leaking.
But more than that, move us to give thanks for the next rainstorm.
Because you are more than a good roof—we need to remember that.
And our neighbors' crops need watering
more than we need to stay dry.

God that madest earth and heaven,

darkness and light

Who the day for toil has given

For rest the night

Guard us waking, guard us sleeping

and when we die

May we in thy mighty keeping

All peaceful lie.

R. Heber

Refuge

Enter and bless this family, Lord, so that its circle will be where
quarrels are made up and relationships mature;
where failures are forgiven and new directions found.

Circle of Love

It is good, dear God, to be a part of this family:
circle of love, place of rest, bastion of peace.
When every other source of comfort fails, this is where I return.
Thank you for being in our midst.

Be Blessed

May you find joy and satisfaction in your family life:
in building a home and setting up a residence—be blessed!
in finding a job and working diligently—be blessed!
in taking care of little ones and making friends in the neighborhood—be blessed!
in seeking God for all your help and guidance, bringing every care to him,
yes, I pray, may you indeed be blessed.

For All of Us

Bless mother and father, sister and brother, grandpa and grandma,
uncle and aunt, and all the cousins.
Here we are in your sight, this family:
May we please you, day by day.

How good and pleasant it is

when brothers live together in unity!

It is like precious oil poured on the head,

running down on the beard,

running down on Aaron's beard,

down upon the collar of his robes.

It is as if the dew of Hermon

were falling on Mount Zion.

For there the Lord bestows his blessing,

even life forevermore.

Psalm 133 NIV

Good Morning

Good morning, God! We greet you with our many morning faces.
We arise sometimes grumpy, sometimes smiling, sometimes prepared,
sometimes behind. Always may we turn to you first in our family prayer.
Bless us today and join us in it.

A Family Prayer

Dear God, for our family we ask your love and care in the days and years ahead. We pray for the strength to go to work every day. It's not easy to get up early and then go out to face the world. The competition is tough, the bottom line inflexible. Give us the strength to work.

We pray for the health of each family member. You know our bodies better than we do. Every ache and pain, every sickness, is a concern to you. Therefore we ask that you keep watch over our bones and muscles and every bodily system, because you are the Great Healer.

We ask for guidance in all the decisions we must make in the days ahead, the big decisions, and even the little daily ones. We acknowledge that without divine direction, our lives become meaningless, wrapped up in our own selfishness, heading nowhere. Lead us where you want us to go!

Let us be friends with our neighbors. Especially give us patience when it seems our comforts are ignored or our rights infringed. In every dispute, let us be willing to be fair, and even take less than we deserve. And give us a spirit of humility that we might offer help and comfort when we see a neighbor in need.

For the students in this family, we pray for extended hours of concentration. We ask that the days of books and classes might be filled with energy and the joy of learning as you provide wisdom and intelligence.

Give us time to play together, to have fun, to laugh. For we know that your dwelling place is a place of joy and laugher. Let us experience in this family a little bit of heaven on earth.

Finally, increase the strength of our bonds of love so that we might bear witness to your love in our community. Give us the desire to offer hospitality at every opportunity. And throughout all our days together, may this family learn to worship better and better, seeing all you have so graciously given us. Amen.

A New Family

We're starting a family, God.
Parenthood: What joy, envisioning the future.
What dreams for a new beginning, a new venture in relationship.
And what sadness . . . for all the free time that will be no more!
Assure us that we can do it, God. By your grace, we know we can. Amen.

Love Lines

*Motherhood is leaving an indelible mark on me, God of new beginnings.
Stretch marks adorn me like a lace gown!*

*So much stretching goes into mothering. We stretch to make inborn nests; to
free these nestlings from our flesh; to feed them. When I squint toward the
future, I envision stretching to help children walk, run, and fly from my
nest. Along the way, keep me flexible, stretchy, and malleable.*

In your hands, stretch marks are love lines on belly, soul, and mind.

Blessing for Our Unborn Child

*Bless this dear child, Lord, being woven from our love.
It, too, is expanding like the body-cradle where the child slumbers,
unknown but already loved. Bless and be with us as we practice
lullabies and prayers, on our knees in joy and awe.*

Hold That Thought

Once the kids arrive, romance gets nudged aside by the
carpool, and candlelit dinners happen only
when the power is out.
Which, we fear, God of love, could happen to us, the
couple who were lovebirds once upon a time.
Help us retrieve the "us" that supports the family,
for we are a union blessed by you.
As we cope with a full house now, remind us of empty
nests ahead, a love-nest time just for us.

Oh, what a happy child I am,

Although I cannot see!

I am resolved that in this world

Contented I will be.

How many blessings I enjoy

That other people don't!

So weep or sigh because I'm blind,

I cannot, nor I won't!

Fanny Crosby, age eight

Tending a Marriage

Marriage, Lord, is like a garden:
You don't keep digging up a plant to see if its roots are growing!
Sustain us, for there are seasons of wilted growth just as
there are seasons of blossom and fruit.
While ripening to become useful, may we love one another
with the same strengthening trust and patience you,
gardener of the world, show toward us.

Monkey See, Monkey Probably Do

In the raising of children, Lord, can I teach what I can't do?
To observe them is to know that they're already developing skills they see me model.
O God, help! To equip them to become the best they can be, I must start with myself.

Message of Giggles

Bless the children, God of little ones, with their giggles and wide-eyed awe, their
awaking assumption that today will be chock-full of surprises, learning, and love.
Neither missing nor wasting a minute, they take nothing for granted, a
message that blesses us. We will go and do likewise.

Children, obey your parents in the Lord, for this is right. "Honor your father and

mother"—which is the first commandment with a promise—"that it may go

well with you and that you may enjoy long life on the earth."

Fathers, do not exasperate your children; instead, bring them up in the

training and instruction of the Lord.

Ephesians 6:1–4 NIV

For the Children

Bless these children, God.
*   Keep them growing in mind and body.*
Keep them ever moving and reaching out
toward the objects of their curiosity.
And may they find, in all their explorations,
the one thing that holds it all together: your love.

Dance of Parents

It's not polite to boast, but to you, knower of innermost thoughts,
I whoop and holler in delight: I love being a parent!
And I am sometimes the best parent around. My children are the finest.

Just a minute . . . I must go tell them.

Despite tiredness and worry, I have moments of sheer,
cartwheeling, rainbow-dancing joy. I hope there are times when you say that of me.
Maybe today? as I join my kids to play in the leaves, make snow angels, picnic,
dance a teen gyration, or share pizza in celebration of just being together.

Take our hands and jump with us for joy!

Living Parts of Speech

All I don't know, Lord, is most apparent when children are around.
Their curiosity is insatiable. I'm grateful I don't need all the answers,
just a willingness to consider the questions and honor the
questioners. Knock, seek, ask are imperative verbs
implying your blessing on our quests.

In the Blink of an Eye

Just yesterday, the children
were babies; overnight,
they have jobs, homes,
and babies of their own.
"Overnight" change, Lord,
is comforting, though, reminding me
that nothing stays the same.
Not tough times, not good ones,
just the blending
of one stage into another.
I am grateful for the movement
with you at my side.

Passing the Love Around

Bless us in this time of play together. Let each child know she is loved.
And let us parents recognize that the love we offer here
is the same affection you have already worked in our own hearts.

The Joy of Giving

May you know the joy of giving
in this family. Not only
on birthdays and holidays,
but every day.
Not only when others are looking,
but when no one will ever find out.
Give, and give again!
For this is the only true route
to happiness, the only road
to lasting peace.

Telling the Family Tale

Thank you for the gift of memory. Playing
"I remember" is such fun, Lord of history, especially the sharing of it with
grandchildren who, like relay runners, are here to
pick up their part of our family tale.

For Our Family

May your eyes look kindly upon this family, Lord,
*   for we need your love and guidance in our lives.*
This is a family that seeks to do the right things—
*   to work hard for a living,*
*   to raise up children who will contribute to society,*
*   and to be a blessing in our neighborhood.*
But we know we need your constant help to do these things.
May we be filled with love and happiness—
all of us who live in this home:
*   by fulfilling our responsibilities, day in and day out;*
*   by being accountable in all our actions;*
*   by giving whenever we can, even when it hurts;*
*   by nurturing warmth and understanding among us.*
And by always looking out for the best interests of others.
Please grant our requests according to your great goodness. Amen.

Blessing a Stepfamily

*Bless this gathering of what, at first glance, looks like mismatched parts,
encircling God, for we want to become a family. Guide us as we* step
*closer to one another, but not so close as to crowd.
Heal wounds from past events that made this union possible.*

*Bless the children with the courage to try new relatives, new traditions,
new homes. Empower them in their anger, helping them know that it is
okay and that tears are healing. Assure them that they have the
strength to live in two worlds and hearts big enough to love others.
Make us, the step-adults, worthy of this love, for it comes at great cost.
Help us respect previous traditions and loves and not* step *too close in our need to
belong. For even in the midst of celebrating, there is mourning.*

Remind us to take baby steps *as we become all you have in mind.
Your presence will be our companion, your love our protection, and
your wisdom our guidance in this awesome responsibility.
Step* closer, *loving God, and lead us.*

Yours, Mine, and Ours:
Blessing for a Stepfamily

We come as pieces of a puzzle that can't quite fit together.
Bless and lead us, a family in the making, God of unity. Turn us around,
sort us out, and reassemble us in a satisfying whole.

Calming the Storm

Bless us as we weather this family conflict. We all have certain needs to be met, certain ways of trying to fulfill our dreams. Yet each of us seeks this one basic thing in the midst of it all: love. Simply love.

Perfect Parent

When our children fall short of the mark and we parents fall farther still, O God, we scold ourselves to do it all, and perfectly. Give us wisdom to know that you don't ask us, nor do the children, to be perfect—just to be there.

Ascribe to the Lord, O families of nations, ascribe to the Lord glory and strength, ascribe to the Lord the glory due his name. Bring an offering and come before him; worship the Lord in the splendor of his holiness . . . Give thanks to the Lord, for he is good; his love endures forever.

1 Chronicles 16: 28–29, 34 NIV

From Parent to Parent

Today I lost patience with my child. Please help me never to do it again, God.
Teach me to see myself just as you see me: a learner still discovering life's wisdom,
still experimenting with right and wrong, still making foolish mistakes.
And help me to be understanding with my child just as you have always
been with me, all down through the years.

Grace for the Family Reunion

We come today, O God, as near strangers gathered from scattered lives, for families no longer live close by. Be the common thread running through our reuniting as we recall and rededicate our ancestors' memory.

Bless us, Lord of history, the next generation, as we take our place as the ancestors-to-be. Bless and guide the young ones, our descendants. Help us be worthy of their remembering.

Through this meal and catching up, embrace us and send us back to our distant homes renewed, refreshed, and revitalized until we once again join hands with you around the family table.

. . . keep your father's commands and do not forsake your mother's teaching.

Bind them upon your heart forever; fasten them around your neck. When you walk,

they will guide you; when you sleep, they will watch over you;

when you awake, they will speak to you.

Proverbs 6:20–22 NIV

Family Resemblance:
On Becoming a Grandparent

Thank you for the gift of ancestral faith. May I, as I take my place in the family portrait as the next generation, continue to keep you, everlasting God, as the centerpiece of our family, for your love is as ageless and steadfast as the wind calling my name. Watch over the grandchildren as you have over me in your special ways. Listen as I call out their names in echoes of those family prayers shared on my behalf through a lifetime of faith-full love.

Graces for PBJ & Prayers for Nighty-night

Scooting over to make room, God of daily bread, the kids and I greet you over our peanut-butter-and-jelly lunch. Bless this, our favorite feast.

Through simple graces to bless childhood fare and bedtime prayers to offer you the day, I'm honored to introduce you to my child. But how can I explain who you are to such a little one as this?

Why did I worry . . . again a little child is leading.

You are, as played back in toddler chatter, simply "dear God." An understanding wise enough to last a lifetime.

Good night.

Good night daylight

and playing trains;

good night books,

and bread and butter

and games of make believe,

and brothers and sisters

and father and mother.

Good night, God.

Take care of us while we sleep,

and you have a good night too.

Amen.

Madeleine L'Engle, *Anytime Prayers*

Grace

Bless this food.
And let it remind us once again that the soul,
like the body, lives and grows by everything it feeds upon.
Keep us drinking in only the good and the pure, for your glory. Amen.

The good neighbour looks beyond the external accidents and discerns those inner

qualities that make all men human and therefore brothers.

Martin Luther King, Jr., *Strength to Love*

Bless These Gifts

Bless, O Lord, these good gifts of food and drink.
Because they have come directly from your hand,
* we know they are already blessed in great measure.*
But may this recognition of your goodness in giving
* add to our joy in partaking.*

Neighborly Blessing

Bless my neighbor today.
But keep me from telling him that
* I've got his good in mind.*
Only let him discover it in my smile,
* in my encouraging words,*
* and in my helping hand.*

I will walk in my house with blameless heart.

I will set before my eyes no vile thing.

Psalm 101:2–3 NIV

A small boy, repeating the Lord's Prayer one evening prayed: "And forgive us our

debts as we forgive those who are dead against us."

Anonymous

Spice Versus Snails

Hammers. Aprons.

Which, God of everyday tasks, is the more important tool for life?
Which to what child? Boy or girl?

We worry about equality for sons and daughters.
Daughters are trained for grooming and gathering,
for tending and nurturing—peacemaking.
Sons are trained for arming and dispatching, for toughness—war.

Is this wise stewardship, Lord?

Help us tend our young ones as if all *children need* all
things to be able to build and nurture, cook and compute. Excel.

Steer us from unknowingly forcing them into roles while the kids are in
diapers. Bold, brave blue for boys; prim, passive pink for girls.

The Color of Worry

My favorite color, God of rainbows and sunsets, should be plaid. I'm woven of multicolored strands: parent, spouse, employee/employer, hobbyist, adventurer, and more descriptions than I can list.

I like this plaid me, except for the black and blue spots.

Stay-home versus work-away parents are in battle, and I'm bruised from the crossfire.

Assure us that kids on either side can be fine, for all sorts of parents have their kids' best interests at heart. Thank you for a colorful multitude of parenting options. Equally needed and valuable. Equally blessed.

Double Duty

I am caught, O God, between my growing-up kids and growing-down parents, and I grieve a double loss. Help me, for my sorrow, like my child-parents, is too heavy to carry alone.

111

111

For Those Who Can't Speak

Bless the pets in this house. I don't
know whether or not they have souls, but
I do know they have needs and emotions,
times of playfulness and times of fear.
Keep them in safety throughout this night.
And give me a compassionate heart and
a caring attitude toward them always.

Bless My Pets

God of beasts and critters, bless them,
for they bless me even when they shed on the
couch and don't come when called.
They love without strings and share the simplest
joys of walks and catnaps in the sun,
slowing me to a pace you recommend.

Bless This Mess

The house is a mess, Lord, and because of it, my
attitude is a matching mood.
Like handwriting on the wall of my
grumpy heart, I got your message:
'Tis far wiser to hunt first crocuses on spring days
than lost socks in the laundry;
to sweep leaves into piles for jumping
than grunge in a corner;
to chase giggles rising from a child's soul
like dandelion fluff than dust balls beneath beds.
Bless, O Lord, this wonderful mess,
and send me out to play.

Bless the Ruts in the Yard

I am grateful, O God, that your standards run more to how we're loving
you and one another than how we appear. If you judged on lawns,
I would be out in the cold!

Mine is the yard where kids gather.

Ball games, sprinkler tag's muddy marathons, snow fort and tree house
constructions, car tinkerings and bike repair—they all happen here.

Bless my rutted, littered lawn, wise Creator. It's the most beautiful landscape,
dotted as it is with children who will be grown and gone faster
than we can say "replant."

115

An Updated Portrait

Bless my family, O God, for it is unique . . . some say too much so.
I am grateful you know we are joined by love—for each other
and for and from you.
We are grateful you use more than one pattern to
create a good family. This pioneering family
has you at its heart.

A Single Blessing

My God, I thank you for the blessings of the single life.

One of your plans was for people to get married and have children.
But I know that your good and perfect will is also for some
of us to live unmarried and not have children.

For this life I thank you. For the gift to be free to learn to love without clinging.
To seek relationships without owning, to offer my love
and kindness among many friends.

Yes, Lord at times I am lonely, like all people can be.
So I ask you to fill those times of emptiness with your presence.
Enter into the barren places with your refreshing water of life.

And as I continue on this path—living by myself—keep my friends and family close,
no matter how far away they live. Give me peace in my daily work,
joy in the pursuit of wholeness, and comfort in the solitary nights.
And please continue to give me a giving heart. For I know, Lord, I am blessed.

CHAPTER FOUR

At Work

Blessed is he who has found his work; let him ask no other

blessedness. He has a work, a life-purpose;

he has found it and will follow it.

Thomas Carlyle, *Past and Present*

Leaving a Mark: A Blessing for Jobs

Bless our work, Lord of vineyards and seas.
We long to leave a mark as visible as a building or bridge.
We yearn to be connected with what we do and to do something that matters.

Show us that what we do is as indelible as a handprint on fresh concrete
even though our mark may be in spots no one can see right now except us.
Harvest comes in its own sweet time.

Bless our left-behind marks, for with you as our foundation, our work is as
essential to the overall structure of life as a concrete pillar.

A Job Well Done

How good to get this promotion!
And how I've waited for this day!
Now that it is here,
I thank you for the chance to savor it.
A job well done is a good thing, I know.
I will celebrate before your smiling eyes and give you credit, too.
Because, after all, everything I am and have
comes from your gracious hand.

Working for Others

May you know, deep within, that all your work is not just for you alone,
but for the common good. And as you pursue your career with so much energy,
may you enjoy the blessing of looking out for those who have no work
to do. Look after them, too. And grant them all the benefits
of your wisdom, should they ask for your help.

Special Tasks

*O God, you have called each of us to special tasks, purposes, and vocations,
equipping us with the skills and energy to perform them.
For some, our vocations send us into the labor force; for some, it is soon
bringing retirement. For some, it is in full-time homemaking.
For some, our vocations are in artistic skills; for some,
in volunteering, helping, neighboring.
Always, there is that first call from you, God of vision,
working through our work to help, heal, change a needful world.*

Healthy Competition

*The surge of adrenaline as we look over our shoulders to see who's gaining
on us is as natural as breathing, Lord, and we pick up the pace to keep
ahead. If behind, we dig in to overtake whoever is ahead of us.*

*Competition is exhilarating, and we welcome its challenges.
Yet, competition out of control creates bare-knuckle conflict within
us, and we are shocked at the lengths to which we will go to win.
Help us weigh the risks and benefits of getting a corner office,
promotion, and raise.*

*Keep us achieving, Lord, for being the best, brightest, and boldest is a worthy goal.
Help us win fair and square and not cheat ourselves. Help us remember that
we can best gain the competitive edge by focusing on your guidance.
And how, really, can we see where you are leading if we are walking backward
on the lookout for whoever might be overtaking us! That is losing, no matter what we win.*

I have learned that success is to be measured not so much by the position that one has reached

in life as by the obstacles which he has overcome while trying to succeed.

Booker T. Washington, *Up from Slavery*

Answering the Call

Work is good right now, God of all labor, and I think I know why:
You and I are working together. Is this what it is to be called?

I think it must be, for you are the source of my talents, for which I am grateful.
Through the support of others, gifted teacher, mentors, and leaders, and
through those willing to take a chance on me despite the odds, you
have always been present, and I am grateful for that, too.

Although this sense that I am doing what you intend for me is usually
just a delicious, split-second awareness, O God, it is enough to keep me
going when I am tired, frustrated, and unclear about my next step.
Our companionship of call to vocation is not an instant process,
but rather a shared journey. Keep me listening, watching.

I am glad we share this working venture, for on the job and off, I am blessed.

As I go through this day, help me to be sensitive to the fears and cares of my fellow workers.

Remind me not to add my grievances and burdens to their own.

Anonymous

The Blessing of Work

What a blessing, Almighty One,
*   to be able to earn a living for the family!*
To be free of worry about what they will eat,
*   or what they will wear,*
*   or where they will sleep.*
You have given so much:
*   house, flowers, table and chairs,*
*   even a video camera to help us remember*
*   these days that are flying by so quickly.*
Yes, you have given.
And your gifts are a serious calling:
Show us how to give in return!

From the fruit of his lips a man is filled

with good things as surely as the work

of his hands rewards him.

Proverbs 12:14 NIV

125

It is observable that God has often called men to Places of Dignity and Honour, when they have been busy in the honest Employment of the Vocation. Saul was seeking his Father's Asses, and *David* keeping his Father's Sheep when called to the Kingdom. The Shepherds were feeding their Flocks when they had their glorious Revelation.

God called the four Apostles from their Fishery, and *Matthew* from the Receipt of Custom; *Amos* from among the Herdsmen of *Tikoah,* Moses from keeping *Jethro's* Sheep, *Gideon* from the Threshing Floor, & c. God never encourages Idleness and despises not Persons in the meanest Employments.

Ben Franklin, *Poor Richard's Almanack*

Slow Down

May you find today
that, rather than thriving
on the hectic pace of your schedule,
just slowing down a bit
can be the greatest of blessings.

Whistling in the Dark

We sing this to the tune of "Downtown," Lord, for a chuckle:
"When you're at work, whether boss or a clerk, you can be . . . downsized."
Laughing lightens the threat while we wait and see if life imitates song.
Be with us, for we're mostly whistling in the dark.

I wonder why it is that when anxiety is such a heavy burden, we go right on reaching for tomorrow's load today. Most of us do. I am sincerely trying, though, and with some success these days, to form the habit of remembering that it was the God of the universe who said you only have to live one day at a time.

Eugenia Price, *Another Day*

Bring Back the Joy

How boring these meaningless details!
Is this really what work is meant to be?
Can you make it sing again?
Put the spark back in my zeal?
Because I know that work is a blessed privilege;
I don't want to be ungrateful.
But how boring the piles of paperwork,
how deadening the countless reports,
how fatiguing the endless round of meetings.
Yes, I need to feel it again, Lord—the joy.
Help!

. . . do not depend too much upon your own industry, and frugality, and prudence, though excellent things, for they may all be blasted without the blessing of Heaven; and therefore, ask that blessing humbly, and be not uncharitable to those that at the present seem to [lack] it, but comfort and help them. Remember, Job suffered, and was afterwards prosperous.

Benjamin Franklin, "The Way to Wealth"

Sleeping on the Job

Achievers, it is said, spend nights
on the office couch snuggled up with work.
Should we all follow suit?
Lord, lead us past the temptation to sleep on the job,
literally and figuratively. Grant us the good sense to know when
to lock up and go home. There's nothing like a good night's sleep
in our own beds, surrounded by snoring family, to get us ready for work
tomorrow, refreshed and eager for your call to excellence.
Goodnight, Lord, time to call it a day.

Out of Steam

I have lost some of my zeal to do the work here, God. Forgive me for falling into despair and for being on the lookout for a greener pasture at the expense of full concentration on the tasks at hand. Help me not to cheat my employer by only giving a halfhearted effort.

But most of all, I want to keep my eyes on you, Lord, not on things or places or the myriad circumstances beyond my control. I know that true happiness and fulfillment will come only from being in your will.

And when it is time to move, you will show me. Therefore, strengthen my faith in your goodness. For I know your commitment to me has never been in question. Your zeal for my life never cools. Praise you!

A Prayer for What It Takes

You invented work, God, and I am grateful.
Framer of the Cosmos, you've given me a project, too.
Creator of the Earth and Oceans, sustain my hands to do it right.
Designer of Amoebas and Atoms, give me pause to look after the details.
Worker of Ultimate Skill, accomplish your masterwork in my soul this day!

Whatever you do, work at it with all your heart, as working for the Lord,

not for men, since you know that you will receive an inheritance from the Lord

as a reward. It is the Lord Christ you are serving. Anyone who does wrong

will be repaid for his wrong, and there is no favoritism.

Colossians 3:23–25 NIV

For This Moment

Bless these next few, short moments in my day, before the next
problem arises. And may I remember, in all my busy-ness,
that the best time to seek you is always the same: now, right now.

Bless My Work

*All work can be good, Lord, for you can upgrade the most mundane,
difficult, or nerve-racking job into one that matters.
God of all skills and vocations, bless and inspire* my *work;
deliver me from boredom and laziness.*

"F" Is for Failure

Miserably, embarrassingly, and very publicly, Lord, I failed at work,
costing the company money and time. Peers sympathize but are mostly
relieved they didn't blunder. Remind me not to gloat the next time
I am successful and someone else wears the dunce cap of failure.
Help me separate what went wrong from who went wrong,
for my efforts were well-intended. Be with me as I walk down the hall,
chin up, face forward to try again. Help me learn from my failures,
and first of all not to believe that I am one.

How Did You Do It?

How can I work in a place like this?
Where people keep fighting over status and power,
where most of the words are unkind at best,
where grasping is the main activity,
lying an everyday thing?
Where the smiling face, the helping hand,
seem jarring in their out-of-placeness?
How could you work in a place like that, Jesus?
How did you do it?

The Most Important Things

Bless this office where I spend so much of my time each day.
In all the work I do, let me never forget my life's true priorities:
family, friends, and the will of God.

The Real Paycheck

I thank you for my work, Lord. And please bless me in it.
Most of all, help me to remember that the paycheck
worth working for consists of more than just money.
It must include meaning and significance,
for myself and others.

Tools

Bless these tools of my work, Lord.
Keep them sharp and strong and ready to do my will.
And bless these hands, too, that they might be ready to do all you desire.

Come now, little man,

turn aside for a while from

your daily employment,

escape for a moment from

the tumult of your thoughts.

Put aside your weighty cares,

let your burdensome distractions wait,

free yourself awhile for God

and rest awhile in him.

Enter the inner chamber of your soul,

shut out everything except God

and that which can help you in seeking him,

and when you have shut the door, seek him.

Now, my whole heart, say to God,

"I seek your face,

Lord, it is your face I seek."

Anselm, "A Call to Meditation"

What About the Kids?

*Childhood is a treasure, and we working parents fear we're squandering it
as we hire strangers to share and mold it. Guide our choices, Lord.
Hold our children in your hand while we're gone.*

Thou, O God, dost sell us all good things at the price of labour.

Leonardo da Vinci

Pulled Apart

*Like the turkey wishbone, God of wholeness, I am being pulled apart by job,
family, home, errands, friends, and my needs. I'm preoccupied with what I
am not doing and feel the pull to do it all.*

*Help me choose wisely. Remind me to negotiate on the job and at home for
the time I need in both places. Remind me, O God, to negotiate with myself
for a leaner lifestyle, for I am part of the pull. In the tugging days ahead, be
the hinge that keeps my life's parts synchronized in harmonious movement,
not split apart at all.*

Revolving Doors

Bless the nannies, sitters, and caregivers who tend our work-a-bye children, Lord, for we leave our greatest treasures in their hands. How difficult it is to drop them off on our way to work beyond home.

Sometimes we feel defensive and guilty under the stares of others who judge our working choices. But we don't make them lightly, and we do our best to ease transitions and soothe tears—both the children's and ours—in the partings. Continue to help us choose wisely; soften criticisms, both those of others and our own.

For whether we are at home all day or not, we are all full-time parents, Lord, worrying, praying, holding our young in thought twenty-four hours a day even if we cannot be by their sides every moment.

So help us, Lord, both the working-away and the staying-put parents, to fully be involved in our children's journeys through our homes, no matter on which side of the front door we spend most of it.

Free men freely work: whoever fears God fears to sit at ease.

Elizabeth Barrett Browning, "Aurora Leigh"

New Direction

Life is full of trade-offs, Lord,
and I need to make one.
I want to venture off the fast track
where I'm losing more
than I'm gaining.
Guide my search for a job
where I can have both a
life and a living.
Restore my balance,
not the checkbook kind,
for it will change when I do.
Your balance is not found
running in a circle,
but along a beckoning path
where enough is more than sufficient;
where money comes second to family,
community, and self; where
success takes on new meaning;
and where, in the giving up,
I gain wealth beyond belief.

Switching Horses Mid-life

A banker is now a nurse, moving at mid-career
from being counter to contributor.
O God, how we envy those who take the risk.

Nudge us to get going; prod us past this middle, which like a seat-sprung rocking
chair has lulled us into settling for being counters when we could be contributors.
Help us learn to tell the difference, for there may be ways to modify where we are.

With your energetic belief in us, Lord, we know there is no better time
than mid-career and mid-life to change course. Middlers have "double vision,"
seeing both behind and ahead, and the view is exciting.
With your help, we see that the glass is more than half full for those
who say, "I know where I've been, and the future looks better than the past,"
and then make a new day happen.

Mid-career, mid-life, is as good a time as any to make a change, Lord,
and certainly better than never.

Blessing for a New Job

May you find your new job to be a source of deep satisfaction.
Here in this office, may creative ideas flow.
Here at this desk, may your mind be stimulated as never before.
And may all your dreams and visions for this good work come to fruition.
For the Lord, too, wants your potential fulfilled in every way.
Yes, may it be!

For a Calling

May the gifts and talents God has given become apparent to you. And with that recognition, may there also arise a clear sense of where to apply them. A career is an important thing. For God's will is your fulfillment; your being in just the right place is the joy of his heart.

Moving On

The new job waits, the old desk is cleared. Be with me, Lord,
as I say good-bye to work friends. Help me find new friends in coworkers as dear
as these. Help me put down roots in new parking spots, behind new desks and equipment.

Remind me each time I look at the farewell gifts I am taking with me today
that nothing is ever lost, no one ever forgotten. May the memory of this place,
these bonds, nourish me tomorrow; today, it is okay to be sad.

Patience

Lord, it's hard to wait for word about my new job. Did I get it? Did they turn me down?
I'm so looking forward to starting, so why the delay? Can't they make up their minds?

Yes, I do need patience more than anything else—and right now!
Please quell my anger and help me see that if this isn't the right place for me,
I can trust you to keep it from me. But it's hard to wait. Still hard to wait.

Making a Choice

Lord, more than half your working children told a survey that,
given a choice, we would take more time over more money.
And it's true, as you know from our sharing concerns and
frustrations with you. We are time deprived.
These days, we would be happiest taking an extra day off
work instead of the day's pay. Amazing.

Are the times a-changing, Lord? Are workaholics becoming
passé and is prestige for working twenty hours a day dimming?
Are we going to have four-day weekends with more
free time to spend as we decide with family, home, self?

Probably not, Lord, for most of us won't have that choice right away.
Most of us will remain secret "time-aholics," yearning in private for more time.
Give us the wisdom to ask ourselves, when this hunger hits,
"more time for what?"

Motivate us to answer in such ways that will goad us to find extra time now,
for even an extra hour here or there would help.
Even five extra hours a week would be enough time to . . . to what?
What do we want to do so badly that we will pay a day's wages to do it?

Guide our search of current schedules to see where we can pluck extra time: mornings? late nights? weekends? Taking just a little from each one could give us a sizable pile of found time to use in new ways. Help us be satisfied with this small step even as we hunger and plan for more.

Urge us to pay attention to our need for more time, for it is a worthy yearning. We need all the time we can get. And at the same time, when we find extra hours, restrain us with a gentle hand if we are tempted to squander any of our precious time doing things that seem hardly worth the effort much less worth swapping for a day's pay!

Thank you for the gift of extra time however, whenever, and wherever we gain it. With your guidance, we will be investing it wisely.

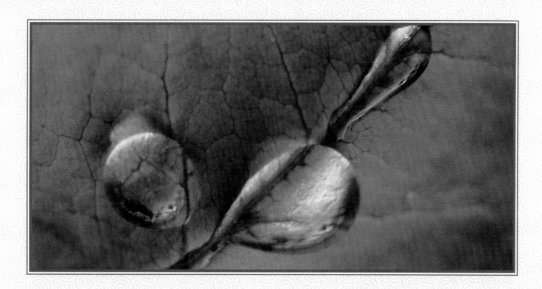

Cubed

We work on islands inside efficient cubes as small as a closet,
private as an elevator, and cozy as a phone booth! Lord,
give us the courage to peek around corners.
We want to take down the walls a notch.
It's not good for folks to live, or work, alone.

Bonds

Sometimes lunchtime on the job feels like a family reunion.
Our coworkers feel like family and we are grateful to belong.

What a blessing to be members of a creative, caring unit—caring
about the business and those who make it happen.
Productivity is up as lifted morale provides the momentum to do
more and do it better, byproducts we take home.

Bless the folks down the hall, across the room, in the next
department, or in the office next door.
They are more than coworkers, they are workaday neighbors.

On the Job Together

Join us at work, Lord, and in our insecurities about it;
getting to and from it; in our triumphs and masteries over it;
and short cuts and temptations through it.
Work, amazingly, is where we spend most of our time.

For the Boss

May you be the leader you were meant to be today.

May you find courage to temper your business goals with an eye toward human compassion.

May you carefully weigh the consequences of every tough decision you make—the effects on the company and the impact on all who work within it.

May you know that one greater than you goes before you and stands behind you, offering great wisdom.

And in this knowledge may you seek to lead just as he did: being servant of all.

Fair Play

How about some help around the house, Lord, where I need your guidance to make homemaking a shared endeavor rather than Mom's Motel? Inspire me with plans to enlist instead of accuse. I'm counting on you to be at the dinner-discussion table and in the kitchen afterward with the new cleanup crew. Time for a shift change.

In the name of the Lord Jesus Christ,
we command you, brothers, to keep away
from every brother who is idle and does not live
according to the teaching you received from us.
For you yourselves know how you ought
to follow our example. We were not idle when
we were with you, nor did we eat anyone's food
without paying for it. On the contrary,
we worked night and day, laboring and toiling
so that we would not be a burden to any of you.
We did this, not because we do not have the
right to such help, but in order to make
ourselves a model for you to follow. For even
when we were with you, we gave you this rule:
"If a man will not work, he shall not eat."

2 Thessalonians 3:6–10 NIV

147

I was too ambitious in my deed,

And thought to distance all men in success,

Till God came to me, marked the place and said,

"Ill doer, henceforth keep within this line,

Attempting less than others"—and I stand

And work among Christ's little ones, content.

Elizabeth Barrett Browning, "Content in Service"

We plow the fields and scatter

The good seed on the land,

But it is fed and watered

By God's almighty hand;

He sends the snow in winter,

The warmth to swell the grain,

The breezes and the sunshine,

And soft, refreshing rain.

All good gifts around us

Are sent from heaven above:

Then thank the Lord, O thank the Lord

For all His love.

Mathias Claudius, "We plow the Fields and Scatter the Good Seed"

Going for the Interview

I have an interview today, O God, and feel inadequate to the task,
much less the job I am being considered for.

First impressions count for much, and I may not be wearing the proper clothes,
attitude, or smile, immediately losing an advantage. I may make silly mistakes,
blundering through facts that I know as well as my own name.

However, Lord, with you at my elbow, I may just as likely be at ease,
competent, and pleasant. Interviews are like spinning coins:
They can fall either way, depending a lot upon how we view and present ourselves.
Help us consult with you about that beforehand.

No matter today's outcome, remind me to look in the mirror
you hold up so that I can see a reflection of someone who did my best.

If nothing else, Lord, this interview will be good practice for others down the road;
nothing is wasted in your world, even bad interviews that can be
redeemed into training sessions for future triumph.

Meeting the Challenge

May you never fear failure in this job.
Push into that fear and go through it.
Let it stimulate you to better methods
as you find new ways to solve old problems.
May you never allow the potential risk
to keep you from trying a good thing.
For this work will challenge you in every way.
It was meant to be that way.
And you were meant to do it.

Seasoned Workers

Ready or not, free time is at hand for some of your finest seasoned workers, Lord,
early retirees downsized, out-sized, and put prematurely out to pasture.
Help us start again, for we are hidden treasures other companies could use.
Remind us as we start the search that even temporary employment is better than sitting
around. Keep us in the workforce, for we, like fine furniture, gain luster with age,
something young folks can't begin to match.

CHAPTER FIVE

Spiritual Insights

Speak, move, act in peace,

as if you were in prayer.

In truth, this is prayer.

François de Salignace de La Mothe Fenelon

A Prayer Primer

We accept your invitation to pray without ceasing.
Hear us as we pray boldly, with expectation, believing your assurance
that we deserve to be in your presence and to talk all we want.
We are grateful that you welcome us at all times and in all places and moods.

God is faithful; he will not let you be tempted beyond what you can bear.

But when you are tempted, he will also provide a way out so that you can stand up under it.

1 Corinthians 10:13 NIV

Hide and Go Pray

I need to talk to you, Lord, but when and where? When life offers few prayable moments, lead me to a quiet spirit spot at work or home or in traffic between the two. Briefly is enough time until we have more.

Be kind to your little children, Lord.

Be a gentle teacher, patient with our weakness and stupidity.

And give us the strength and discernment to do what you tell us,

and so grow in your likeness. May we all live inthe peace that comes from you.

May we journey towards your city, sailing through the waters of sin

untouched by the waves, borne serenely along by the Holy Spirit.

Night and day may we give you praise and thanks, because you have

shown us that all things belong to you, and all blessings are gifts from you.

To you, the essence of wisdom, the foundation of truth, be glory for evermore.

Clement of Alexandria, *To the Divine Tutor*

Prayer for a Seeker

God grant you the joy of learning, as you seek spiritual direction.
Listen to those who are wise in the ways of the spirit.
Hear the inner workings of your own heart.
And grow closer to God.

God's Will

When life goes awry, Lord, I need someone to blame
so I point the finger at you. Heaven help me,
I want it both ways: you as sender and fixer of trouble.
Help me know you don't will trouble, for what could you possibly gain?
And when the good you want for me isn't possible in the
randomness of life, I know you are with me.

Running

Running is so good.
Can muscles silently praise you?
I catch a vision of life's goodness in the pounding of my feet,
*   even in the sweat pouring down.*
You made this warm machine, and you gave me the responsibility
*   to keep it going.*
I will pray now, with energy, exertion—gutting it out.
But I will not pray with words for awhile.
For you are here as I pick up speed.
And what, after all, needs to be said aloud at this moment?

Right Now

Let me do what lies clearly at hand, this very minute.
Grant me the insight to see that too much planning for the future
removes me from the present moment. And this is the only existence,
the only calling I have been given—right now to do what is necessary.
Nothing more, nothing less. Thus may I use this next moment wisely.

Most of us don't pray on a regular basis

because we're deeply aware that it will cost us something.

More than time.

More than money.

More than faith.

More than becoming religious.

To lay hold of prayer as my own available resource for effective,

practical, daily use—as an abiding certainty in an

unpredictable world—will cost me one thing.

Honesty.

Jack W. Hayford, *Prayer Is Invading the Impossible*

Discovery

O God, I am guilty of transgressions that make
me ashamed, and I fear you'll leave me. Yet have you ever refused
to forgive those who ask? Why would I be different?
Reassured, I accept forgiveness and will share it
with those who need it from me.

Blessing for This Night

The day has been long, Lord, but that's water under the bridge.
Bless me now with stillness and sleep. I sigh and turn over, knowing that
night will usher in the day with new joys and possibilities,
gifts from your ever-wakeful spirit.

All through the Bible we see God's patience and perseverance as He pursues

misguided and obstinate men and women—men and women who were born to a

high destiny as His sons and daughters, but who strayed from His side.

From Genesis to Revelation God is constantly saying to such,

"Return to me, and I will return to you."

Incredible as it may seem, God wants our companionship.

He wants to have us close to Him. He wants to be a father to us, to shield us,

to protect us, to counsel us, and to guide us in our way through life.

Billy Graham, *Till Armageddon*

Blessed Friendship

May you come to know
that God is your friend.
When you feel a frowning face
is looking down at you from heaven,
recall that nothing you could do
could ever make God love you more
or love you less. He simply loves—
completely, perfectly.
So feel the blessedness of that!

Lord, dismiss us with thy blessing,

    Hope, and comfort from above;

Let us each, thy peace possessing,

    Triumph in redeeming love.

Robert Hawker, "Benediction"

161

Around the Bend

I'm getting a crick in my neck trying to see around the bend, God of past and future.
I'm wearing myself out second guessing.
Teach me to live in today, needing just a small glimpse down the road.
No need to borrow trouble that may not be waiting.

Worthy of Worship

So many things will offer themselves to me for "worship" today.
But reveal yourself, God, in all your creativity, as the only being worthy
of my true adoration.

Answers

We pray but don't feel answered, Lord. Help us understand
that regardless of the answers we want, being connected to you through
prayer is changing us into "can do" people. We can find solutions,
we can try again. Looking back, we understand you did answer.

Free Love

You love us Lord, not because we are particularly lovable.
And it's certainly not the case that you need to receive our love.
I am so heartened by this:
You offer your love simply because you delight to do it.

Zapped

Tree or person, lightning can topple whatever it hits.
Console us with your truth that trouble, trauma, tragedy—like lightning—
just happen. Random and without malice from you. Should it strike, we'll
look for rainbows, assured of your presence as we pick up the pieces.

Faith makes all evil good to us, and all good better; unbelief makes all good evil, and

all evil worse. Faith laughs at the shaking of the spear; unbelief trembles at the

shaking of a leaf, unbelief starves the soul; faith finds food in famine, and a

table in the wilderness. In the greatest danger, faith said, "I have a great God."

When outward strength is broken, faith rests on the promises.

In the midst of sorrow, faith draws the sting out of every trouble,

and takes out the bitterness from every affliction.

Robert Cecil (1563–1612)

164

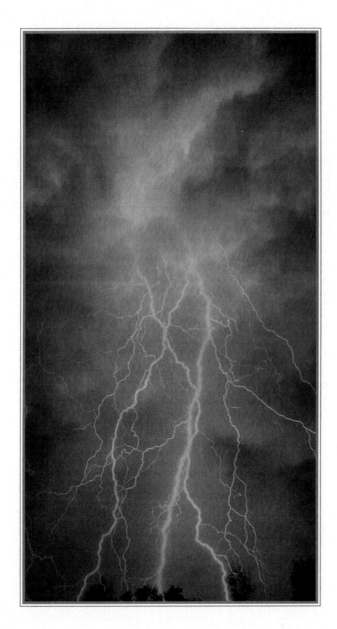

Yet, in the maddening maze of things,

And tossed by storm and flood,

To one fixed trust my spirit clings;

I know that God is good! . . .

I know not where His islands lift

Their fronded palms in air;

I only know I cannot drift

Beyond His love and care.

John Greenleaf Whittier, "The Eternal Goodness"

God

God.
God is.
God is holy.
God is personal and close.
God is there; God is here.
God is spirit.
God is.
God.

More Than Meets the Eye

*May you know that a wisdom and a love transcend the things you will
see and touch today. Walk in this light each step of the way.
Never forget that there is more to this existence than the material
side of things. And be blessed when you suddenly become
aware of it: in the smile of a child, in the recognition of your own soul's
existence, in the dread of death, and in the longing for immortality.*

This Shall Not Pass

*May you learn to let your happiness depend, day by day, not upon something
you could possibly lose, but upon that which could never, ever pass away.*

Satisfaction

*Comfort us, God, when we come to this awesome conclusion:
What did not satisfy us when we finally laid hold of it
was surely not the thing we were so long in seeking.
Yes, comfort us by this recognition:
In all our longings, we are only yearning for you.*

Four stages of growth in Christian maturity

Love of self for self's sake

Love of God for self's sake

Love of God for God's sake

Love of self for God's sake.

St. Bernard of Clairvaux

Why Take Time to Pray?

Time is tight, Lord, and I wonder why I bother to pray.
The question is answer enough: I need a relationship where I don't have
to bluff and hurry. And when I pray boldly? I offer myself as a possible
answer to prayer. No time to waste.

Why Am I Here?

I come to church today, not because of duty or because a preacher calls, but because you, O God, invite me, your child, for whom you've been searching. In the words and songs, the lights and symbols, I feel, like a pulse, your spirit beating within me.

Accepted

May you know deep in your heart that God is not in love only with what he hopes to make of you in the years ahead. He is simply in love with what you are—right now—a forgiven, perfectly accepted human being.

If God is for us, who can be against us? He who did not spare his own Son,

but gave him up for us all—how will he not also, along with him, graciously

give us all things? Who will bring any charge against those whom God has chosen?

It is God who justifies. Who is he that condemns? Christ Jesus, who died—

more than that, who was raised to life—is at the right hand

of God and is also interceding for us. Who shall separate us from the love of Christ?

Shall trouble or hardship or persecution or famine or nakedness or danger or sword?

As it is written:

"For your sake we face death all day long: we are considered as sheep to be slaughtered."

No, in all these things we are more than conquerors through him who loved us.

For I am convinced that neither death nor life, neither angels nor demons, neither

the present nor the future, nor anything else in all creation, will be able to separate

us from the love of God that is in Christ Jesus our Lord.

Romans 8:31–39 NIV

What's in a Word?

We are, as the Psalmist says, wondrously made.
So much so, loving Creator, that by changing our minds we might
be able to change our lives. It's the simple power of as if.
Living as if *we are going to fail, we often do. Living* as if *we are going to*
succeed, we often can. Keep us from being like teams who know
the plays but doubt they can run them.
Instead, we'll use your amazing gift of attitude, knowing you
treat us as if *we deserve your promised abundant life.*

The Blessing in Your Eyes

When you look around you today,
know the blessing of seeing God
in every smiling face.
Reflect that blessing in your own eyes,
silently with a kind heart.

Oh, the depth of the riches of the wisdom and knowledge of God!

How unsearchable his judgments,

and his paths beyond tracing out!

Who has known the mind of the Lord?

Or who has been his counselor?

"Who has ever given to God,

that God should repay him?"

For from him and through him and to him are all things.

To him be the glory forever! Amen.

Romans 11:33–36 NIV

Sunday Morning

We find ourselves here in the pew because somewhere in our lives, clearly or muffled, we heard you call. Here we are, sleepy and alert, worried and assured, certain and doubtful, to hear your message fit for us all.

Is there any Duty in Religion more generally agreed on, or more justly required by God, than a perfect Submission to his Will in all Things? Can any Disposition of Mind, either please him more, or become us better, than that of being satisfied with all he gives, and content with all he takes away? None, certainly, can be of more Honour to God, nor of more Ease to ourselves; for if we consider him as our Maker, we dare not contend with him; if as our Father, we ought not to mistrust him; so that we may be confident whatever he does is for our Good, and whatever happens that we interpret otherwise, yet we can get nothing by Repining, nor save any thing by Resisting.

Benjamin Franklin, *Poor Richard's Almanack*

Summing It Up

*Children sitting at your knee, Great Teacher, we're collecting footnotes
of faith wisdom: In prayer, grumbling is good; in stress, grieving is essential;
and in trouble, redeeming grace is promised. In that truth, we'll not drudge
through life but rather fly like skiers down a powdery slope.*

Weed Power

*Even in our toughest moments, Lord, we yearn to grow into fullest flower.
Give us a faith as resilient and determined as dandelions pushing
up through pavement cracks.*

173

Morning Prayer

Bless us, Lord, as we go to worship this morning. Look down upon our efforts to honor your name through song and word and fellowship.

And help us do it. For only in your power do we live and move. And in your being alone we find our true identity.

Come, let us sing for joy to the Lord:

let us shout aloud to the Rock of our salvation.

Let us come before him with thanksgiving

and extol him with music and song.

For the Lord is the great God,

the great King above all gods.

In his hand are the depths of the earth.

Psalm 95:1–4 NIV

The Worthy Pursuit

We are far too easily pleased, Lord. We run after our toys with such vigor.
We pursue every form of recreation, as if it could somehow save us.
We involve ourselves in relationship after relationship, hoping that each
     new conquest will give us full satisfaction.
We work and work, earning more and more money, thinking that somehow
     happiness can be bought, or that the joy of the future can be mortgaged today.
We multiply the objects of our amusement and the means of our entertainment,
     believing that if we can only turn off our minds for
     a few hours, our true situation will disappear into the background.
Yes, we are far too easily pleased with all we can do for ourselves.
But how much energy would we exert toward obtaining our true Home
     if we could only see the place you've prepared for us?
Give us that vision, God, and the determination to reach for your promises every day.

God's plans, like lilies, pure and white, unfold;

We must not tear the close-shut leaves apart;

Time will reveal the chalices of gold.

Mary Louise Riley Smith, *Sometimes*

A Prayer for the Right Words

*Thank you, God, for the wisdom to know when to speak,
what to say, and how to say it. Guard my mouth today from any form of
foolishness, that in all circumstances I might honor you with my words.*

Sound Sleepers

*Security, loving God, is going to sleep in the assurance that you know our
hearts before we speak and are waiting, as soon as you hear from us, to
transform our concerns into hope and action, our loneliness into
companionship, and our despair into dance.*

True Leaders

We have been guilty, Lord, of looking for our leaders only in the places of wealth and influence. We confess a fascination with power. We want to glorify the outwardly successful, passing over those who have learned to live wisely and with true integrity. Rather, we tend to follow after those who give blithe answers with the appearance of absolute confidence.

But you have offered us better, we know.

Your plan for us is that we follow those who follow the right and the good.

Your spirit fills those who walk in humility, patience, and self-sacrifice. Please open our eyes that we may see those gentle faces beckoning us upward and onward in a spirit of love. They are all around us, we're certain. Only open, open our eyes!

Star Signs

To those scanning a night sky, you sent a star. To those tending sheep on a silent hill, you sent a voice. What sign, Lord, are you sending me to come, be, and do all you intend? Let me hear, see, and accept it when you do.

Mirror, Mirror

We're too hard on ourselves, God of truth.
We see only the blemishes like teenage "zits" that erupt on a chin
instead of the smiles, the laugh lines, the bright eyes,
some of our best qualities.

We give ourselves depressions over who we are not and starve ourselves
into life-threatening illnesses trying to fit into someone
else's ideas of how we should look.
Which, by the way, isn't all that cute.
We copy and imitate, we nip and tuck, we dye and lie.

Help us out here. What do you think when you assess us?

You say we are created in your image, which tells us
something right away: We are special. You say we are salt
that gives life its savor, that we are lights on hills to beckon and illumine. You
say we are called by name even before we are born, that even the hairs of our
heads are numbered. From the very beginning, you have said that everything
you created—which includes us—is "very good."

It's hard to believe. Yet, we know, Lord, that who we say we are affects our
relationship with you. If we feel unworthy, unlovable, we shy away from
approaching you. Too often before we come talk to you in prayer, we act like the
folks who tidy up the house before the cleaning service comes.

We are learning differently, and here we are, the real us.

Bless this authentic us with our approval, for it is surely
more accurate than the mirrors that fickle society, the here-and-gone-again

fads, the please-love-me
celebrities, and the buy-me,
buy-me commercials hold
up for us. All of them are selling
products and images that require
us to see ourselves as losers,
as "less than" we are.
You, on the other hand,
O God, are handing out a free
message that we are your beloved,
beautiful, handsome, and very,
very special children just
as we are. Now this
is an image to live up to.

179

Silent Prayer

Bless me with silent conversations, O God, so I may be with you while doing chores, while singing in the shower, while brushing the cat. Sometimes words don't have to be spoken to be understood, and I get your message, too, in the silence that fills and comforts.

. . the Spirit helps us in our weakness. We do not know what we ought to pray for, but the Spirit himself intercedes for us with groans that words cannot express. And he who searches our hearts knows the mind of the Spirit, because the Spirit intercedes for the saints in accordance with God's will.

Romans 8:26–27 NIV

Best Friend

Know this: Prayer is quite informal,
one heart communing with another, with or without words.
If we make it any more complicated than that,
have we not insulted our very best Friend?

Listening for God

Lord, we've tossed our prayers aloft, and hopefully, expectantly, we wait for your
  answers. As we do, we will:
  listen, for you speak in the voice of nature;
  see you as a companion in the face and hand of a friend;
  feel you as a sweet-smelling rain, a river breeze;
  believe you can provide encouragement, direction, and guidance for those who have
  only to ask.
  We feel your presence.

People of God

Coming together in worship with prayer, song, and psalm makes us expectant people.
Here we find what we came seeking: your abiding, ever-present daily love.
We leave, blessed with the truth that it goes with us into the rest of our lives.

Missing the Mark

Lord, it's hard to hit a target with closed eyes, yet I approach you blindly. Help me see
that faith is not a quantity that can be measured like gas in a tank but a gift,
a quality, that says, "I believe God is for me, not against me."

Morning

God, you are so great.
It is always the right time to worship you, but morning is best.
Praise for the dawning light that streams in through this window.
Praise for the sound of the birds as they flit through in the air.
Praise for the little spider crawling along on the ceiling.
Praise for the smell of coffee and the warmth of a cup in my hands.
Praise for the flowering plants—and even those weeds growing by the house.
Praise for the neighbors walking along the sidewalk and the clouds moving
  by, too.
Most of all, praise for the breath that keeps flowing in and out of my lungs.
Yes, this is the greatest item of praise: that you alone are my life—all life
  itself.
Without you, all is dust.
Praise . . . for you.

Kneeling to Pray

Your changes touch my life with hope and mystery. God of love and power, I come today ready and eager to experience your power working through me.

Call to Action

We know, Lord, that action is the proper fruit of knowledge and all spiritual insight. But so often we wish only to think and muse, without ever doing good toward anyone.

Yes, it's easier to know *the good than to* do *it.*

It's more comforting to be right than to do the right thing.

It's more convenient to sit on the sidelines and give advice than it is to enter the game.

It takes less energy to tell others how to carry their burdens than to take up a share of the load with them.

But we need to be shaken out of our lethargy, God. We need to recognize that our lack of love is evident in our lack of good deeds. We need to see ourselves, so often, just as we are: sometimes selfish, often lazy.

Change us, God! Open our eyes that we may see the needs around us. Show us the poor—and all the ways we can help. Bring us to the sick—giving us words of comfort and creative means of succor. Let us no longer pass by the hungry stranger, but move us to offer what is in our hand and in our cupboard to share.

Help us to take the more difficult route of service.

Help us to forsake the ease and comfort of a purposeless life.

Help us to make friends with the unlikable, to bond with those who are different.

Help us to take all we know and put it into every resource at hand, so that action may result for the good of all.

For if you will show us that we, too, are poor and hungry, feeble and needy in so many ways, then we will recognize that our giving can only spring from what we have already been given.

CHAPTER SIX

Healing Prayer

A cheerful heart is good medicine.

Proverbs 17:22 NIV

How Does Faith's Garden Grow?

In the dead of winter, God of springtimes, I'm gardening.
Carrot tops rooting, sweet potatoes vining. I don't doubt the outcome since
I've learned at your knee to live as if. As if useless can become useful;
as if seemingly dead can live; as if spring will come.

With Solomon, I will rejoice "See! Winter is past . . .
flowers appear on the earth; the season of singing has come,
the cooing of doves is heard in our land."

How does a winter garden grow?
With hope. It grows brighter each time I live
as if, knowing that you, O God, color even our
wintry days from love's spring palette.

The Lord bless you and keep you;

the Lord make his face shine upon you and be gracious to you;

the Lord turn his face toward you and give you peace.

Numbers 6:24 NIV

189

Now on his way to Jerusalem, Jesus traveled along the border
between Samaria and Galilee. As he was going into a village, ten men
who had leprosy met him. They stood at a distance and called out
in a loud voice, "Jesus, Master, have pity on us!"

When he saw them, he said, "Go, show yourselves to the priests."
And as they went, they were cleansed.

One of them, when he was healed, came back, praising God
in a loud voice. He threw himself at Jesus' feet and
thanked him—and he was a Samaritan.

Jesus asked, "Were not all ten cleansed? Where are the other nine?
Was no one found to return and give praise to God except this foreigner?"

Then he said to him, "Rise and go; your faith has made you well."

Luke 17:11–19 NIV

Birds of a Feather

Troubles, dear Lord, have cast us loose from assumptions and certainties,
and we are bobbing like rudderless boats on a stormy surf.
When all hope seems gone, we spot doves on the horizon.
Doves like those you sent your Noah children to assure them the storm
was nearly over. Doves in the phone calls from friends; in the smile
of a neighbor; in the wisdom of caregiver and counselor; in good laughs
or hearty, cleansing tears; in the flash of a new idea, a goal, a dream.

We recognize landmarks now and can see our way through the storm,
guided by your love-winged messengers.

Let Me Be a Healer

I wish to extend my love, Lord.
So give me hands quick to work on behalf of the weak.
Cause my feet to move swiftly in aid of the needy.
Let my mouth speak words of encouragement and new life.
And give my heart an ever-deepening joy through it all.

Great Physician

We don't really know why we have to get sick, Lord.
We only know your promise: No matter where we are or what
we are called to endure, there you are in the midst
of it with us, never leaving our side. Not for a split second.
Thank you, Holy One.

A Blessing for Healers

Bless those who tend us when we are ailing in body, mind, and soul.
They are a gift from you, Great Healer, sent to accompany us along the
scary roads of illness. Bless their skills, potions, and bedside manners.
Sustain them as they sustain us, for they are a channel of your love.

How good it is to sing praises to our God,

how pleasant and fitting to praise him!

He heals the brokenhearted

and binds up their wounds.

He determines the number of the stars

and calls them each by name.

Great is our Lord and mighty in power;

his understanding has no limit.

Sing to the Lord with thanksgiving.

Psalm 147:1,3–5,7 NIV

Binding up a Broken World

You created your world as a circle of love, designer God, a wonderful round globe of beauty. And you create us still today in circles of love—families, friendships, communities.

Yet your circle of love is repeatedly broken because of our love of exclusion. We make separate circles: inner circle and outer circle; circle of power and circle of despair; circle of privilege and circle of deprivation. We need your healing touch to smooth our sharp edges. Remind us that only a fully round, hand-joined circle can move freely like a spinning wheel or the globe we call home.

Our Prayer Is for the Sick

Bring your cool caress to the foreheads of those suffering fever.
By your spirit, lift the spirits of the bedridden and give comfort
 to those in pain.
Strengthen all entrusted with the care of the infirm today,
 and give them renewed energy for their tasks.
And remind us all that heaven awaits—where we will all be whole
 and healthy before you, brothers and sisters forever.

Bless My Doctor

Her hands are so gentle and skilled,
Her mind so quick,
Her heart so filled with compassion.
Bless her in all her duties,
 and in her free time, too.
For she needs physical and spiritual refreshment these days,
 and you, Great Physician, are the one who can help her the best.

After Loss, Going It Alone

Time helps, Lord, but it never quite blunts the loneliness that loss brings.
Thank you for the peace that is slowly seeping into my pores, allowing
me to live with the unlivable; to bear the unbearable.

Guide and bless my faltering steps down a new road.
Prop me up when I think I can't go it alone;
prod me when I tarry too long in lonely self-pity.

Most of all, Kind Healer, thank you for the gifts of memory and dreams.
The one comforts, the other beckons, both halves of a healing whole.

Depending on You

Remind us, Lord, that you dwell among the lowliest of people.
You are the God of the poor, walking with beggars, making your home
with the sick and the unemployed. Keep us mindful always that no
matter how much we have, our great calling is to depend on you—for
everything, every day of our lives.

A Lesson in Suffering

May I be blessed in this suffering.
May I know that you can use this thing to show me
  a mistaken attitude,
  a destructive behavior.
In that way, may I be blessed in this suffering, O Lord, my God.

A Blessing for the Earth

Bless the soil beneath our feet, the sky overhead, and make us one with it.
We are catching on, catching up with ourselves, creator God, and
catching a whiff of the garbage we're burying ourselves beneath. Catching, too,
a glimpse of the fading streams and trash-strewn seas we have long ignored.

Bless and use our reclamation efforts, for it is a task we can't accomplish alone.
With your help, we can bind up and reclaim this poor old earth.
We feel whispers of hope in the winds of changed hearts and minds, for we
recall your promise to make all things new—even this earth we shall yet
learn to tend. We are grateful for another chance.

Listen to what Jesus says to you: "Come to me, all you who are weary and burdened, and I will give you rest. Take my yoke upon you and learn from me, for I am gentle and humble in heart, and you will find rest for your souls. For my yoke is easy and my burden is light" (Matthew 11:28–30). Countless people throughout the ages have discovered this is true—and you can discover it as well as you cast your burdens on Christ. Don't give in to depression and despair—God has a plan for your life.

Billy Graham, *Answers to Life's Problems*

What to Do?

Someone I care about is suffering, Lord, and I feel helpless.
Assure me that a little means a lot and that I'm sharing your healing
love in my notes and visits. If you need me to do more, send me.
I am like dandelion fluff, small but mighty in possibility.

Let Me Help

Help me to see with new eyes today—especially the burden of care that others harbor within them. Grant me insight to see beyond smiling faces into hearts that hurt. And when I recognize the pain, Lord, let me reach out.

To keep me from becoming conceited because of these surpassingly great revelations,

there was given me a thorn in my flesh, a messenger of Satan, to torment me.

Three times I pleaded with the Lord to take it away from me. But he said to me,

"My grace is sufficient for you, for my power is made perfect in weakness."

Therefore I will boast all the more gladly about my weaknesses, so that Christ's power may

rest on me. That is why, for Christ's sake, I delight in weaknesses, in insults, in

hardships, in persecutions, in difficulties. For when I am weak, then I am strong.

2 Corinthians 12:7–10 NIV

Taken With a Grain of Sand

We are surprised by joy, God of re-creation, when we see despair outwitted by simple acts of love as small as grains of sand.
Keep us searching, believing, and building upon them, realizing that grains of sand make dune, shore, and desert.

201

It Is Blessed to Receive, Too

Being ill lately has been difficult. Having to accept from others all the time!
But you have shown me, Good Lord, that unless I am open to others' gifts,
I deprive them of all the pleasure of offering.

We can give touch and comfort and strength in physical healing, but for spiritual healing we need to turn to God. So, knowing our strengths and our weaknesses, we turn to the Lord because all of us carry our past hurts, and He has the remedy for everything. It's simple: If we just turn to Him, He will bring us this inner healing, this spiritual healing so we can make our lives more holy and more pleasing to God.

Sister Dolores, quoted by Mother Teresa of Calcutta, *A Simple Path*

Support Group

This is a club no one wants to join, Lord, its membership dues are high:
trouble, illness, loss. Bless all who share and support.
Like your loaves and fishes, their courage multiplies and
feeds all who come in need.

A New Day

Everything looks much brighter than it did
* before.*
My prayer for strength has been answered.
My cries for help have been heard.
My pleas for mercy flew directly to your throne.
Now I'm ready to help my neighbor, Lord.
Let me not delay.

In Thanksgiving

Finally, I've emerged from the dark night.
Into the light with new energy,
renewed vigor,
a body that responds again.
Thank you for recovery and wholeness.
And bless me as I tell others how good you are!

Reflections of Light

Held up to your light, our broken hearts can become prisms that scatter micro-rainbows on the wall. Our pain is useless as it is, redeeming God, just as a prism is a useless chunk of glass until light passes through it. Remind us that the smallest ray of sun in a shower can create a rainbow. Use our tears as the showers and your love as the sun. Looking up, we see the tiniest arches of hope in the lightening sky.

Sunshine

Headlines tell a dark sorry tale, God, and depress us about
money problems, strife, drugs, and school problems; about housing,
wildlife, family, and health problems.

Trouble is so news-making we forget the rest of the story.
We need sunshine to bring it to light.

Send the sun's light through creation: surf and skyline merging,
bird song and flight. Send it through people: friends who laugh at our jokes,
family who never stray. Send it through inner knowing: unexplained peace
and joy, faith that you're working alongside us.

Reading between the lines of the gloom-and-doom true stories, Lord,
we celebrate your *truth and stretch tall with gladness in the sunshine.*

The greatest disease in the West today is not TB or leprosy; it is being unwanted,

unloved, and uncared for. We can cure physical diseases with medicine,

but the only cure for loneliness, despair, and hopelessness is love.

Mother Teresa of Calcutta, *A Simple Path*

Prayer for Healing Squabbles

We come, needing your help to move beyond:
the times we hurt one another and
the times we willingly misunderstand, cherishing our differences and
the times we assume we know all there is to know about each other and
*   turn away.*
And then there are
the times that we make private rules only to publicly condemn anyone who
*   fails to abide by them, limiting one another by labeling, interpreting,*
*   conditioning, insisting, resisting, defining.*
From all this, Lord, we come, asking that you forgive us as we forgive those
*   "others" we need new eyes to see and ears to hear. Be with us as we do so.*

Body and Soul

May you be healed, in mind, body, and soul.
May you come to know that all healing proceeds from God, and he cares
*   about every part of you.*
Perhaps the healing will come sooner for your attitude than for your body.
Perhaps your mind will experience peace quicker than bones and muscles.
But sooner or later, all will be well.

A Little Means a Lot

*O God, healing is going so-o-o-o slowly, and I am impatient and
grumpy. Mind, body, or soul, this could take a long time.
Remind me that recovery is a journey, not a hasty jet-lagged arrival.
Bless me with faith to sustain me, step by small step.
You do miraculous things with faith as tiny as mustard seeds that,
in time, blossom into awesome growth.
I hold that picture as I make mustard-seed progress
along the road to healing.*

The Lord has done great things for us,

and we are filled with joy.

Restore our fortunes, O Lord,

like streams in the Negev.

Those who sow in tears

will reap with songs of joy.

He who goes out weeping,

carrying seed to sow,

will return with songs of joy,

carrying sheaves with him.

Psalm 126:3–6 NIV

Ordinary Miracles

*When we doubt your miracle-making power, Lord, show us the ordinary
miracles of seasons, of hope regained, of love from family and friend, and of
surprises that turn out miraculous simply by remaking our lives.*

Nourishing Tears

Thank you, Lord, for reddened eyes. Believing your promise that comfort follows mourning, we bawl and sob. In your wisdom, onion-peeling salty tears differ from cleansing grieving ones; we're grateful for their healing.
Deliver us from stiff upper lips, and if we've lost our tears, help us find them.

God the Healer

Please, Comforting Spirit, show me what it means
to let go the hope that others will be my cure.
You, Great Physician,
be my healer in this quiet hour.

Nothing Personal

Strengthen our resolve, O God, to take better care of ourselves, for we eat, drink, and choose risky lifestyles and then want to blame you!
As we live with our consequences, help us know you as the loving parent who weeps first when your children get themselves into trouble.

Present Blessings

May your thoughts focus much more upon what you have
than what you lack *in this trying time. May your heart lay hold of
present realities rather than future possibilities.*

*For this moment—the now—is all we are given.
Whether we are sick or healthy, this juncture in time is the
place we share. Let us be blessed in this moment, needing nothing to
change. Let us simply* be *in God's presence, just for this moment.*

Hopeful Night

*In the midst of mourning life's troubles,
you come to us. In the darkness,
your spirit moves, spreading
light like a shower of stars against a
stormy night sky.*

Flipping a Cosmic Coin

My anger is all consuming and my fantasies are flamed
by satisfying thoughts of revenge. Then, like a rustle of wind across
a wheat field, I hear you reminding me that healing from
violence is an issue of ecology.

Is seeking revenge putting my time and energy to good use? Dear Lord,
I am down on my knees with this one: Shall I rebuild or retaliate?

Healing Memories

How blessed are the good memories, Lord!
In fact, I am beginning to see that
my happiness can consist largely in the looking back.
For that I am thankful, as I lay here, unable for the moment to be active.

New Math for Recovery

Illness requires new math, O God, subtraction *of old fears and* addition *of new thought. Help me bring this lesson home as I draw ten stick figures, color the percentage said to recover from this ailment, and write my name on the brightest figure! A most deserving child, I praise you for the resources to make it happen. Sharing with you* divides *my troubles and* multiplies *my healing chances.*

The little cares that fretted me,

    I lost them yesterday,

Among the fields above the sea,

    Among the winds at play, . . .

among the hushing of the corn,

    Where drowsy poppies nod,

Where ill thoughts die and good are born—

    Out in the fields of God.

Anonymous, *Out in the Fields*

What Is

Today may you come to acceptance.
What is, is.
May you find blessed relief in
    seeing—without judging,
    being—without having to become,
    knowing—without needing to change a thing.
Then, should you be healed, it will be a gracious, unexpected surprise.
May you soon arrive at perfect acceptance.

CHAPTER SEVEN

Renewal

Open wide the windows of our spirits and fill us

full of light; open wide the door of our hearts,

that we may receive and entertain Thee with

all our powers of adoration.

Christina Rossetti

Renew Us

These are exciting times to be part of your world, O God, for your spirit is stirring us into vision and action to revitalize our communities. Be with us in difficult times of decision-making. Still the shrill voices of opponents, for we must learn to be united, despite our differences of opinion.

Move us beyond our too-busy schedules, our boredom with routine and committees, our uneasiness in the face of change, and our preference to debate, delegate, and deliberate rather than do. Be with us as we volunteer and vote. Be with and bless us, the ordinary citizens, the salt of the earth, the "every person," for we are as needy as our streets and communities. Needy in spirits that sometimes falter and sigh under the enormity of the task, needy in energy that is so often drained, needy in vision that is sometimes unclear.

Extend your hand of grace and bless us as we revitalize our neighborhoods, communities, and country, keeping you as cornerstone and Master Builder.

The Lord is my shepherd, I shall not be in want.

He makes me lie down in green pastures,

he leads me beside quiet waters,

he restores my soul.

He guides me in paths of righteousness

for his name's sake.

Even though I walk

through the valley of the shadow of death,

I will fear no evil,

for you are with me;

your rod and your staff,

they comfort me.

You prepare a table before me

in the presence of my enemies.

You anoint my head with oil;

my cup overflows.

Surely goodness and love will follow me

all the days of my life,

and I will dwell in the house of the Lord forever.

Psalm 23 NIV

A New Day is Dawning

*We toss and turn, God of nighttime peace, making lists of
"must do" and "should have done . . . or not" and wind up feeling
unequal to the tasks and sleep-deprived to boot.*

*Bless us with deep sleep and dreams that reveal us as you see us:
beloved, worthy, capable. At dawn, help us see possibilities on our lists.*

*Each time we yawn today, Lord—for it was a short night—we'll
breathe in your restorative presence and exhale worries.
Tonight we'll sleep like the sheep of your pasture, for we lie down
and rise up in your care, restored, renewed, and rested.*

Blessing of Wisdom

Blessings upon you.
The blessing of perfect acceptance
*   in the face of daunting circumstances.*
The blessing of contentment and peace
*   while the winds blow and the waves rise higher and higher.*

Blessings upon you.
The blessing of knowing when acceptance must turn to action
*   for the sake of all concerned.*
The blessing of strength to forsake contentment and peace
*   for the purpose of comforting another.*

Blessings upon you.
The blessing of discernment:
*   to recognize when to wait,*
*   and to understand when to move.*

You have made us for yourself and our hearts are restless until they rest in you.

St. Augustine of Hippo, *Confessions of St. Augustine*

River and Sky

Move our hearts with the calm, smooth flow of your grace. Let the river of your love
run through our souls. May my soul be carried by the current of your love,
towards the wide, infinite ocean of heaven.

Stretch out my heart with your strength, as you stretch out the sky above the earth.
Smooth out any wrinkles of hatred or resentment.
Enlarge my soul that it may know more fully your truth.

Gilbert of Hoyland (twelfth century)

Forgiveness

Let me know the satisfaction of forgiving today, O Lord.
I have held my peace, doused my anger.
Now it is time to extend my hand.

Laughing Through Tears

Thank you for the funny bone, Lord, placed next to hearts broken by
anxiety and fear. A good belly laugh is a gift from you, expanding and
healing heart, lungs, and mind.

Blessed Solitude

May you recognize today
that not all being-alone is loneliness,
and not all solitude is a problem to solve.
With everyone far away,
rejoice in the blessing of quietness.

Grains of Hope

When trouble strikes, O God, we are restored by small signs of hope found in ordinary places: friends, random kindness, shared pain and support. Help us collect them like mustard seeds that can grow into a spreading harvest of well-being.

Moved to New Life

When I freeze in worry and indecision, fill me with the trusting contentment of a child swinging on a garden gate in arcs of slow, free motion. Your presence is oil for the hinges.

Getting a Move On

Like an itch that won't let up, a buzz of creativity is catching our attention and wanting release. Songs whisper to us, wanting melodies; words and paintings are needing paper; dances, our moving feet. Help us recognize your presence in this nudge to movement.

In Stillness

I know that faith is what keeps me moving forward.
But sometimes, too, my trust allows a leisure like this.
For you, God, are the one who upholds all things.
Even as I sit here in stillness,
your breath keeps me breathing,
your mind keeps me thinking,
your love keeps me yearning for home.

Fanning the Flames of New Life

Tossing leaves onto a fire, we name them as regrets and failures from which we choose to be free. We trust you to redeem even these, our deadest moments. They, like autumn leaves, can make the brightest blaze.

Stir new possibilities into life from the embers; fan the sparks of dreams so that we may become one with your purpose for us. It is the root from which we, leaf and human life, begin and from which the most amazing new creation can burst into being, a flame in the darkness.

Create in me a pure heart, O God, and renew a steadfast spirit within me.

Psalm 51:10 NIV

Once, in my imagination I was taken down to the bed of the sea, and saw there green hills and dales that seemed to be clothed with moss, seaweed and stones. And I understood that if a person firmly believes that God is always with man, then even if he is thrown into the depths of the sea, he will be preserved in body and soul, and will enjoy greater solace and comfort than all this world can offer.

Julian of Norwich, *Revelations of Divine Love*

The Lord is the everlasting God,

the creator of the ends of the earth.

He will not grow tired or weary,

and his understanding no one can fathom.

He gives strength to the weary

and increases the power of the weak.

Even youths grow tired and weary,

and young men stumble and fall;

but those who hope in the Lord

will renew their strength.

They will soar on wings like eagles.

Isaiah 40:28–31 NIV

Advent Miracle

Into the bleakest winters of our souls, Lord, you are tiptoeing on tiny infant feet to find us. May we drop whatever we're doing and accept this gesture of a baby so small it may get overlooked in our frantic search for something massive and overwhelming.
Remind us that it is not you who demands lavish celebrations and strobe-lit displays of faith. Rather, you ask only that we have the faith of a mustard seed and willingness to let a small hand take ours. We are ready.

In the Stillness, a Blessing

Bless me with your gifts of silence and stillness. Neglecting to listen for your still, small voice, God of whispered messages, I talk and do too much.

Waiting

So here I am, waiting.
I have answered your call to pray.
I have heard your guidance—to sit tight.
I have chosen quiet and rest because that is your will for me now.
I am sitting on the sidelines, watching the hectic pace around me.
I am finding contentment in the little blessings that flow into my days.
I am trying to see all these things as big blessings because
    they come from you.
But when can I get going again?
When will I do the great works I've envisioned?
When will the situation require dedicated action once again?
When will I hear the trumpet call?
When will I finally move onward and upward?
I'm ready Great Spirit!
Here I am . . . waiting.

Blessing for Peacemakers

Bless me with the kind heart of a peacemaker and a builder's sturdy hand, Lord, for these are mean-spirited, litigious times when we tear down with words and weapons first and ask questions later. Help me take every opportunity to compliment, praise, and applaud as I rebuild peace.

Cheering Section

Bless those who mentor, model, and cheer me on, Lord, urging me toward
goals I set, applauding as I reach them, and nourishing me to try again
when I don't. Remind me to be a cheerleader.
I plan to say thanks to those who are mine.

Fresh Air

Today I need your help, God,
feeling the need for a breath of fresh air.
The old habits and attitudes
I've clung to for so long
seem stale and worn out.
Renew me from the inside out, starting now!

Who am I?

Always a fad behind, I chase elusive fashion trying to keep up with images
I'm told I should resemble. Give me the common sense to revamp what
needs it: attitude, habit, ethics, schedules. Returned in your reflection,
I look fine just as I am.

Praised be You, my Lord, through our Sister Mother Earth, who sustains us, governs us,

and who produces varied fruits with coloured flowers and herbs.

Praised be You, my Lord, through Brother Wind and through

the air, cloudy and serene, and every kind of weather.

Praised be You, my Lord, through Sister Moon and the stars in heaven:

you formed them clear and precious and beautiful.

Praised be You, my Lord, through Brother Fire, through whom

You light the night and he is beautiful and playful and robust and strong.

Praised be You, my lord, with all your creatures, especially Sir Brother Sun, who is the

day and through whom you give us light. And he is beautiful and radiant with great

splendours and bears likeness of You, Most High One.

St. Francis of Assisi, "The Canticle of Brother Sun"

Well-Earned Rest

Lord, bless this time of recreation.
May we see that it is much more
than another form of employment.
It is a time to pull back and relax,
to honor a thing you highly value—
after work: rest.

233

A Spirit of Newness

God of Easter surprises, bring back to life friendships faded because of hurt feelings, marriages broken from deceit, love crushed by meanness. In the doing, hope glimmers like dawn's first sun ray and thaws even the most frozen heart.

Seek God's Goodness

Let the simple life take you by the hand today, and seek the goodness that only God can put in your heart. Be blessed and warmed in his life-giving presence!

The Courage to Be

I wish to be of service, Lord.
So give me courage to
put my own hope and despair,
my own doubt and fear
at the disposal of others.
For how could I ever help without
first being, simply . . . real?

Be the eye of God dwelling with you

The foot of Christ in guidance with you

The shower of the Spirit pouring on you

Richly and generously.

Alexander Carmichael, "Carmina Gadelica"

235

On the Other Hand

I see a robin's egg hatching, Lord, and am set free from my doubts and fretting.
For, while life is not always filled with joy and happiness,
I know it is always held in your hand.

I Am Listening

Dear Lord, I need renewal in my life.
But tell me what you want me to be, first,
then tell me what you want me to do.
Speak, for I am listening,
Guide, for I am willing to follow.
Be silent, for I am willing to rest in your love.

By the reading of the Scripture I am so renewed that all nature seems renewed around

me and with me. The sky seems to be a purer, a cooler blue, the trees a deeper green,

light is sharper on the outlines of the forest and the hills and the

whole world is charged with the glory of God.

Thomas Merton, *The Sign of Jonas*

236

Signs of Hope

We know you, Lord, in the changing seasons: in leaves blazing gently
in fall beauty; in winter's snow sculptures. We know you in arid
desert cactus bloom and in migration of whale and spawn of fish and turtle.
In the blending of the seasons, we feel your renewing, steadfast care,
and worries lose their power to overwhelm.
The list of your hope-filled marvels is endless, our gratitude equally so.

Prayer for a Renewed Heart

Today I want to spend time with you, Renewing Spirit.
In fact, I'd like to spend the whole day just being in your presence.
For this one day I will not worry about the work I
have to do or the goals I want to accomplish.
I will pull back and simply listen for your guidance.

I'm willing to change my life in order to fit your perfect will,
and I ask that you begin that work in my heart, even now.
I'll let go of personal ambition, for now.
I'll loosen my grip on the things I've wanted to
accomplish and the recognition I've craved for so long.
All of this I give over to you.

I'm content to be a servant for now, quiet and
unnoticed, if that is what you desire.
I'm even willing to be misunderstood, if you will only
respond to my sincere prayer for a renewed heart.
Thank you. I need you so much.

God is the friend of silence. Trees, flowers, grass grow in silence.

See the stars, moon and sun how they move in silence.

Mother Teresa of Calcutta, Quoted by Kathryn Spink in *For the Brotherhood of Man Under the Fatherhood of God*

God of the granite and the rose,

Soul of the sparrow and the bee,

The mighty tide of being flows,

Thro' countless channels, Lord, from Thee.

Elizabeth Doten, *Reconciliation*

239

Simply Sitting

O God, my days are frantic dashes between have to, ought, *and* should. *There is no listening bone in me. Lead me to a porch step or a swing, a chair or a hillside where I can be restored by sitting, Lord, simply sitting. With you there to meet me, sitting places become prime places for collecting thoughts, not to mention fragmented lives.*

Because of You

Lord of my heart, give me a refreshing drink
from the fountains of your love,
walking through this desert as I have.
Lord of my heart, spread out before me
a new vision of your goodness,
locked into this dull routine as I was.
Lord of my heart, lift up a shining awareness
of your will and purpose,
awash in doubts and fears though I be.

There is a sense in which a man looking at the present

in the light of the future, and taking his whole being into account,

may be contented with his lot: that is Christian contentment.

—But if a man has come to the point where he is so content that he says,

"I do not want to know any more, or do any more, or be any more,"

he is in a state in which he ought to be changed into a mummy!

Henry Ward Beecher

In the Dark

I know that my character is what I am in the dark,
when no one is watching,
and no one can see.
For this reason, bless me in my solitude.
Because temptation is the greatest here,
and the possibility of a setback looms large.

Puddle Prayers

Pardon my muddy feet, God of raindrops and wriggle worms. I've been outside.
Splashing in puddles like a child is to rediscover your creation: cloak of fog,
spiderweb weavings, birds of different feathers dining
peacefully together. I get too busy to enjoy it.
Thank you for this mud-luscious day when I am brought
to my knees in awe, the best place to meet you—as
any child knows. I plan to pray barefoot from now on, curling
my toes and stretching toward you, becoming like a child, as you
encourage, so each day can be a whole-body experience.
For it is because you are, that I am.

The Gift of Optimism

Enliven my imagination, God of new life, so that I can see through today's troubles to coming newness. Surround me with your caring so that I can live as if the new has already begun.

Weather Forecast

We are blessed by your enveloping spirit as near to us as daily changing weather. Your comfort touches us like gentle rain and hushed snow. And, like the sound of thunder and glimpse of searing lightning, you startle us with new opportunities.

Pure and Lovely

Whatever is right and pure,
excellent and gracious,
admirable and beautiful,
fill my mind with these things.

Too much of the world
comes to me in tones of gray and brown.
Too great the temptation
to indulge obsessive thoughts and sordid plans.

Guard my mind; place a fence around my motives.
The pure, the lovely, the good—Yes! Only those today.

Transformation

May you be made perfect today—with the ability to see clearly your own imperfections,
to accept them fully, and to try with all your heart to transform them for the good.

Topsy-turvy

What a day. When all else fails,
rearrange the furniture.
Lend a shoulder, God of change, as I scoot the couch to a new spot. Like
wanderers to your promised land, I need a fresh perspective. My life has
turned topsy-turvy, and I need a new place to sit . . . first with you, then the
rest of my world of family, friends, job. I need to be prepared for whatever
happens next, and nothing says it like a redone room. I smile as I take my
new seat; this is a better view.

Slowing Down

You heard my prayers to ease my pell-mell race through life, and I am
changing. Only you could teach this old dog new tricks. I feel your
companionship in walks and exercise, in contemplation and prayer. I'm
enjoying this new pace you set.

Pawprints

Winters can be long, Lord, as I've complained before, and hope elusive.
Thank you for sending me outdoors. My spirit soars at the sight of a woodchuck
waking from winter sleep. I rub sleep from my eyes, grateful for signposts
of change, like pawprints in the mud, leading me to springs of the soul.

The True Excitement

When I'm bored, remind me:
This is the excitement of life—
darkness alternating with light,
down dancing with up,
and inactivity being absolutely essential
—as prelude—
to the most fulfilling experiences of all.

CHAPTER EIGHT

Times of Transition

It is only when men begin to worship

that they begin to grow.

Calvin Coolidge

Winds of Change

Spirit of God, keep teaching me the ways of change and growth.
Like the wind, you cannot be tracked or traced.
The breezes blow where they will: silently, invisibly, with great power.
Just as you are working in lives even now.
Let me know your calling as you move in me!
Yes, whisk with your persistent prompting through all the
windows of my soul, the dark corners of my heart.

Lord, you know better than I know myself that I am growing older,

and will some day be old. . . .

Release me from craving to straighten out everybody's affairs. . . .
With my vast store of wisdom it seems a pity not to use it all, but you know

that I want a few friends at the end.

. . . seal my lips on my own aches and pains—they are increasing, and my love

of rehearsing this is becoming sweeter as the years go by. . . .

Keep me reasonably sweet. I do not want to be a saint—some of them are so hard

to live with—but a sour old woman is one of the crowning works of the devil.

Anonymous, *Prayer of an Aging Woman*

Un-nesting Instinct

Thank you, Lord, for the gift of distance as children grow up and away. I'm ready to go on, too. My empty lap is eager for projects that will delight nest-flown children during brief stopovers, all of us too content going on to linger mournfully in our past.

Trapeze Artists

Drawn like moths to flame,
kids lead us new places. Guide me,
pathfinding God, for I'm an
aerialist leaping from bar to bar.
For seconds, I'm holding neither old
nor new: It's impossible to grasp a
second bar while holding the first.
Parents understand.
We can't embrace kids' growth while
requiring them to stay the same.
Help me teach my kids how to
swing on their *bars—have*
standards, goals, a living faith.
Steady me as I help them soar,
for holding them back says
I think they can't.
No matter what today is like,
tomorrow will be different.
Help me, and the kids,
live grace-fully in between.

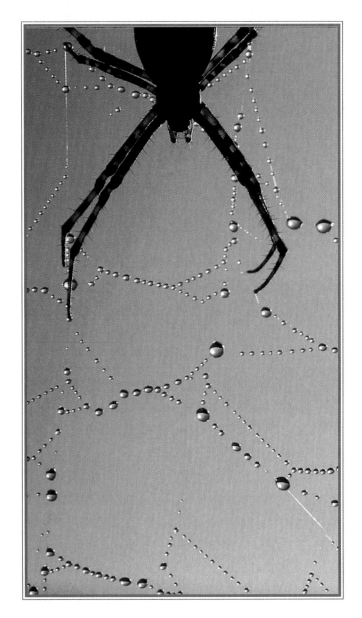

Today First

In this time of change, help me to be patient, God.
Let me not run ahead of you and your plans.
Give me courage to do only what is before me and to keep my focus on my
* responsibilities.*
I am tempted to daydream about the future;
however, the future is in your hands.
Thus, may I be close to you in all my thoughts,
accomplish the task before me today,
and do it with all my heart.

Grace for Being Suddenly Single

I've set a single place at the table, O God, and am dining alone this first
time without my companion, my friend.

What can we say to bless this lonely meal? What words can we use to grace
this half-portion of life? Be with me as I swallow around lonely tears. Bless
my remembering; inspire me to care for myself in honor of all the love that
went before. From now on, I will set places in my heart for Memory and
Hope, new companions for my table.

Suddenly a Family

May you fall in love with this new family more and more each day. No, you weren't planning to suddenly have children, but here they are—a gift from your new spouse. A stepparent isn't accepted right from the start, so be patient. Love will grow between you as you look out for one another's inner needs. Blessings upon you and the children. God grant that you be all a family can be.

Show me your ways, O Lord,

teach me your paths;

guide me in your truth and teach me,

for you are God my Savior,

and my hope is in you all day long.

Remember, O Lord, your great mercy and love,

for they are from of old.

Remember not the sins of my youth

and my rebellious ways;

according to your love remember me,

for you are good, O Lord.

Psalm 25:4–7 NIV

Staying Put

To move or not to move: a riddle for your mobile children. Lord, give us wisdom to know when to go, when to stay, for moving is not always progress, any more than staying is always stagnating. Ease hand-wringing worries and lead us to wise decisions.

Empty Rooms

Finally, my children all have homes of their own.
So this house feels so much bigger.
I know it can become
a cold and lonely space or a warm, comforting haven.
You will make the difference, Lord.
Pack these rooms with all the good memories,
until the next time my children visit,
bringing their children, too, along with them.

As a very small boy exploring the almost virgin woods of the old Carver place,

I had the impression someone had just been there ahead of me.

Things were so orderly, so clean, so harmoniously beautiful. A few years later in this same woods I was to understand the meaning of this boyish impression. Because I was practically overwhelmed with the sense of some Great Presence. Not only had someone been there. Someone was there.

Never since have I been without this consciousness of the Creator speaking to me.

George Washington Carver, *Carver of Tuskegee*

Students of Re-creation

Hold my hand, O God, I have a school stomachache.
First day of school.
Bless your many "mature" students and give us an A+, for we found the courage to detour from unfulfilling jobs, inertia, or life changes to answer a call to become, do, more by returning to school.
Bless our role in your re-creation. The burr under the saddle to go, do, is a gift from you, the Creator who inspires dreams and provides resources to reach them. That's a lesson I'm excitedly learning.

A Transitional Prayer

May your nerves hold out in this transition!
It's hectic making big changes. It takes away the security, the comfort, the sense of stability.
We were made for change, but we prefer the status quo. We even begin to assume that
where we make our home can be heaven itself. But there is only one true heaven.
And may your nerves hold out until you arrive!

No one should give the answer that it is impossible for a

man occupied with worldly cares to pray always.

You can set up an altar to God in your mind by means of prayer.

And so it is fitting to pray at your trade, on a journey,

standing at a counter or sitting at your handicraft.

St. John Chrysostom

The Next Step

Lord, give me the faith to take the next step, even when I don't know what lies ahead. Give me the assurance that even if I stumble and fall, you'll pick me up and put me back on the path. And give me the confidence that, even if I lose faith, you will never lose me. Amen.

Not Overnight

Dear God, help me see that aging, like being born, happens one day at a time. Calm my fears that it will overtake and overwhelm me. Help me briefly mourn youth as only a butterfly cocoon that must crumble to set the new creature free.

Problems, Problems

You have made things problematic again, Lord, and I need to see that all this upheaval can be a good thing. Help me, Lord. And thank you for showing me that a thoroughly comfortable existence can rob me of real life.

THE BODY

of

BENJAMIN FRANKLIN

printer

Like the cover of an old book,

Its contents torn out,

And stripped of its lettering and gilding

Lies here, food for worms;

Yet the work itself shall not be lost,

For it will (as he believed) appear once more,

In a new,

And more beautiful edition,

Corrected and amended

By the AUTHOR

Benjamin Franklin, *Epitaph on Franklin's tombstone*

Respite

I celebrate the gift of contentment,
knowing there is no guarantee it will last.
But for now, it's great to rest—just to rest in this wonderful calm.

Rejoice in the Lord always. I will say it again: Rejoice! Let your gentleness be

evident to all. The Lord is near. Do not be anxious about anything, but in

everything, by prayer and petition, with thanksgiving, present your requests to God.

Philippians 4:4–6 NIV

Just Enough

In this time of great change, help me, God of tomorrow, tomorrow, and
tomorrow, to trust your guiding presence. Inspire me to follow in the
footsteps of ancient desert nomads who wore tiny lanterns on their shoes to
give just enough light for the next step. All I really need.

What we love we shall grow to resemble.

St. Bernard of Clairvaux

First Morning Grace

We are now one, Lord of commitments and pleasures. Just as wind fills sails and removes clouds to create sunny days, be a constant presence each day of our marriage. Bless this first breakfast. We are grateful for it and your gift of one another.

Growth Rings

O Lord, Bless our life stages, for they read like growth rings on a mighty tree:

our beginnings and firsts with their excitement, newness, and anxiety;

our middles, full of diligence and commitment and, yes, we confess, sometimes boredom, but also risk and derring-do;

our "nexts," the harvests and reapings; the slowing down and freedom. In your hands this time can be rich and full like an overflowing cup, not a last or a final or an empty or an ending stage at all.

You are an Alpha and Omega God, the parentheses between which we live, move, and have our being. Bless our comings and goings.

Retirement

Retirement presented me with a watch that ticks only in free time. Guide me as I commute on the wings of prayer from old days to new ones where I'm a rookie again. First day on the job, Lord, of savoring my investment of well-earned time. Let's spend it joyously.

Grandchildren at the Goal Line

*Once again, a little child is leading. I had become so serious all I
knew were tasks behind, tasks ahead—until the grandbaby threw me
a ball to chase. There I went, like some silly old fool. But chase it I
did, catching baby laughter on the air like delicate, iridescent bubbles.
Thank you, Lord, for the gift of play returned to me in the hands of
grandchildren. Keep me agile and ready to drop whatever task is
tethering me to routine and follow where I am led, even across a goal
line scuffed in the driveway dust.*

The older I grow, and I now stand on the brink of eternity—the more comes

back to me that sentence in the Catechism I learned when a child,

and the fuller and deeper its meaning becomes:

"What is the chief end of man? To glorify God and enjoy him forever."

Thomas Carlyle

Blessing for Old Age

Bless my milestones from first grandchild to last day in my own home and, dear Lord, the ordinary days between. Bless my tears, for they nourish new fields where I find joy in the harvest. Bless my aging, a rebirth into who you yet call me to be.

Making New Places for God

Change is inevitable, Lord, we know.
Help us to accept: If we view each transition
as an opportunity to experience your faithfulness,
then we make new places in our lives
for spiritual growth.

Prayer for a New Employee

May you enjoy your new job. Slide into it with a calm heart. Find the pencil sharpener. Don't become overwhelmed with all your new responsibilities. God can help you approach each task, one at a time, starting on your very first day. Look to him, and your new friends, for all you need. Blessings!

I stood up straight and worked

My veritable work. And as the soul

Which grows within a child makes the child grow,

Or, as the fiery sap, the touch of God,

Careering through a tree, dilates the bark

And toughs with scale and knob, before it strikes

The summer foliage out in a green flame—

So life, in deepening with me, deepened all

The course I took, the work I did.

Elizabeth Barrett Browning

267

First Grace in a New Home

Join us for a meal, Lord, on our makeshift table of boxes and leftovers of our old life as we make a new home. May your love, like the logs we brought from the old tree back home to lay on a new hearth, be the spark we need to make this move one of growth and success. Be with us in our lonely, homesick moments; guide us to new neighbors so that our daily bread may once again be the nourishing center for friends. Bless this crackers and cheese meal, Lord; it is first communion in a new start.

In a New Place

May God grant that you will find happiness in your new destination—
in the transition from country to city: peace.
in the move from friends to strangers: acceptance.
in the letting go of the old to embrace the new: confidence.
in the challenge of new work: unflagging zeal.
In all these ways, the blessing of God be upon you.

Of Life and Risk

May you remember that life was never meant to be risk-free. And let this be your comfort in the days ahead: You are not the first to walk this fearful path, and you will not be the last. But everyone who comes and goes here is precious to the Lord and proceeds only under his watchful eye.

Grace to Welcome a New Baby

The new baby sits centerpiece proud on the dining table as we eat a sleepy, still incredulous meal. Where before there were only two at our table, now there is a family eating together. Only you, Creator God, could come up with such a marvel, and we are awed even in the midst of exhaustion and newness. May our family dinner conversations in the years to come nourish and fill as we continue the creating you have begun, the making of a family.

Blessing New Parents

*May you find that starting a family was your best decision ever.
Look into the eyes of this little one and be blessed.
You're due to receive a lot of love.
Only be sure you give even more in return.*

Don't let anyone look down on you because you are young, but set an example for

the believers in speech, in life, in love, in faith and in purity.

1 Timothy 4:12 NIV

270

Grace for the First Day of School

We've brought this child sitting across the breakfast table as far as we can go alone, Lord. Now we must share the pleasure, the task, with others. Be with us, for it is hard to stand aside, opening the door upon a world of knowledge, peers, and farewells where parents can't go. Bless this special explorer; may your ever-vigilant love support and nurture this young mind as the food before us now does the body. Rejoin us at supper tonight, Lord, for we'll have much to share with you.

Transitions

May you let your longings for home spur you on:
to make new friends,
to start new projects,
to dream new dreams.
Times of transition are difficult.
But the energy of making the move
can be channeled into something so positive.
May you find this true in every way as you pull up the stakes.

Don't Be a Stranger!

May you leave home with a good feeling in your heart.
Fond memories,
a willingness to write,
a desire to return for friendly visits.
You are loved here.
Don't be a stranger!
May you cut the apron strings, though, as you need to.
Growth is our wish for you.
And this is God's plan for you, too.
Receive his blessing!

A Grace for Dieting

Are there graces for lettuce, Lord? And low-fat, no-fat, meat-free, fun-free meals? I need you to send me words for blessing this paltry meal, for it's hard to feel grateful for these skimpy portions when all I think of are the foods not on my plate. Help me change that thought, to make peace with choosing not to eat them, for I need help in becoming the healthier person I want to be. Hold up for me a mirror of the new creation you see me becoming, for I need a companion at this table.

I stoop

Into a dark tremendous sea of cloud,

It is but for a time: I press God's lamp

Close to my breast: its splendour, soon or late,

Will pierce the gloom: I shall emerge one day.

Robert Browning, "Paracelsus"

Setting Out

*As you leave home now, may you know that your whole family
will be keeping you in their thoughts and prayer.
Let this sustain you in the tough times; let it keep you
anchored in the joyful times, too.*

*Seeing you launch out on your own is so good!
Enjoy the blessing of independence, and come home whenever you can.
The welcome mat is out, the porch light on. And our same
God will take care of you, just as he has watched over us all, for all these years.*

There is a time for everything, and a season for every activity under heaven:

a time to be born and a time to die, a time to plant and a time to uproot,

a time to kill and a time to heal, a time to tear down and a time to build,

a time to weep and a time to laugh, a time to mourn and a time to dance,

a time to scatter stones and a time to gather them, a time to embrace and a time to refrain,

a time to search and a time to give up, a time to keep and a time to throw away,

a time to tear and a time to mend, a time to be silent and a time to speak,

a time to love and a time to hate, a time for war and a time for peace.

Ecclesiastes 3:1–8 NIV

Graduation Day

Have you noticed, Lord, that we've been seeing only the back of our student's head these days? The head that today is proudly wearing the crown of accomplishment, its tassel blowing in the wind of movement into a future you both created. Today is just the next step into it.

Not-So-Empty Nest

An empty nest. Finally!
Now it's time for some fun:
dinner and dancing,
long walks in the park,
visits with old friends,
full concentration on fulfilling work,
a round of golf,
and a little fishing, too.
I never thought it would be so calm and quiet around here.
What a blessing. And thank you, God!

Gone but Not Forgotten

The funeral flowers are fading, O God, but not the presence of this special one still with me in memory. As long as I have it, shared time is not ended, merely continued. Thank you for this gift. It will make bearable the solitary days ahead.

A Birthday Prayer

*God of endings and beginnings, what joy to celebrate another happy
return of my day. Give me courage to face what waits
unseen ahead and what remains behind.
At the turnstile of a new birthday year, I am excited and ready.*

Mother-in-Law Joke

*In the toss of rice at a wedding, I've become the punch line of a joke:
I am, heaven help me, a mother-in-law.*

*I am looking to you, Wise One, for guidance as I reinvent myself.
I creak like a rusty joint as I move over to give the new
mate space in my family alongside my child.*

*Nudge me into a gentle background role of part mother, part friend,
part historian, and part wise woman who bites her tongue and
trusts the reshaping process. In it, may I be a resource to
call upon, not a caricature to resent.*

Second Marriage

Give me many years with this dear new mate, O God, so that I can piece them together in a quilt of second married love, a wedding gift from you.

From Here to There

What joy to move from here to there!
What a sense of excitement and anticipation!
What a brand-new outlook—leaving behind the old, familiar places!

Going Someplace New

Bless my bump of curiosity, God of all good gifts, for following it, as a child
chases after a floating balloon, is like reading a turning page:
movement to somewhere else.

Far-sighted

Give me a hint, steadfast God, about what lies ahead,
for I want to see around the corner to the future.
If that's not possible, help me live as if the future is now,
assured that each day's grace will be sufficient.

Looking to the Future

I know I'm going to yearn for the days past;
I'm sure of it.
I can feel the lump in my throat
and the tightness in my chest
when I think about how safe and settled I was—back there.
Why do we have to move? Why all the upheaval?
Or is it required of me so I might grow?

CHAPTER NINE

Life Lessons

Though man sits still and takes his ease,

God is at work on man;

No means, no method unemploy'd

To bless him if he can.

Edward Young, "Resignation"

It's Tempting

*Lead me not into temptation, O God, the daily ones, like keeping
money I find, or exaggerating a headache into an excuse,
or leaving racist remarks unchallenged.
Small temptations, are they too trifling to worry about?
It is tempting to think so, for I could easily go from occasional to habitual,
from small to big. Keep me consistent in what I say and do, consistent in
resisting temptations strewn before me by a world that says,
"Come on, just once . . . just a little . . . won't hurt."
Stay nearby, I feel a little weak-kneed.*

Over mountains

and over valleys

and over oceans

and over rivers

and over deserts

one says: Blessed are You, Lord,

    our God, king of the world,

    who makes the works of creation. . . .

Over rain

and over good news

one says: Blessed are You, Lord,

    our God, ruler of the world, who is

    God and who does good things.

And for bad news

one says: Blessed are You, Lord,

    our God, ruler of the world,

    who is the true judge.

The Talmud, Blessings, Berakhot 9:2

285

Taking Care of Today

*Slow my pell-mell race into the future, everlasting God, for I am racing
past the exquisite moment which, like a snowflake, is
unlike any other and never to be retrieved.*

A Resounding Shout

Love. It seems so simple. Love is a gift given. Yet, if we don't overlook it,
Lord, we treat it like a gift certificate saved so long it expires.
We are down-on-our-knees grateful your gifts of love and grace never expire.
Nudge us to use them, for we lose their value each day they go unclaimed.
We stay disconnected from you, the source of creation and re-creation.
To connect only requires a "Yes!" from us. Hear us shout!

Being Within Being

Blessed is the one who can look upward and recognize divine glory
in the sun and clouds, who can look downward and be moved to praise
by stones and flowers.

Blessed is the one who can look inside and find Being within being,
knowing she is never alone, certain there is more
to be known than to be seen.

Giving In

*Help me to remember, Lord, that I have not won an
argument simply because my friend is remaining silent.
I'm beginning to see that I have won nothing
until I consider giving in.*

*Help me do just that in this tough situation.
I know it won't be easy, but keeping a friend is hard work.
That's why friendship is such a valuable thing.
And it's why I am so thankful to have it. Help me—help me loosen my
grip on this one thing. For the sake of my friend and for your sake.*

A Second Look

Give me eyes, O God, to take a second look at those who think, act, and look different from me. Help me take seriously your image of them. Equip me with acceptance and courage as I hold out a welcoming hand knowing that you are where strangers' hands meet.

Father God, thank You for my many friends who stand beside me in all situations.

They are always there when I need them to listen, laugh, and cry.

They are so special to my life. May they realize what their friendship means to me.

Amen.

Emilie Barnes, *15 Minutes Alone with God*

Imperfect

*Only machines run perfectly—for awhile—and we know exactly
what to expect from them. But we are different, Lord.
We often do the unexpected, certainly the imperfect.*

*Give us the joy of diversity, the pleasure of indulging variety in our approaches to life.
Being incomplete, we reach our hands to you, expecting help. And that is good,
since only in you can we be perfectly fulfilled.*

Opting for Hope

Given a choice between hope and despair when trouble hits, Lord, I pick
hope. It doesn't trivialize suffering or dismiss evil, it simply trusts your
promise to make all things new.

Hope writes the poetry of the boy, but memory that of the man. Man looks forward

with smiles, but backward with sighs. Such is the wise providence of God. The cup

of life is sweetest at the brim—the flavor is impaired as we drink deeper, and the

dregs are made bitter that we may not struggle when it is taken from our lips.

Ralph Waldo Emerson

Of Love and Vulnerability

May you avoid the temptation to treat love as a mere commodity today.
It is a most precious gift, bound up within the soul of another.
It can only be given and received at the price of great vulnerability.
Blessings upon all who know it, really *know it.*

Holy God, you have shown me light and life.

You are stronger than any natural power.

Accept the words from my heart

That struggle to reach you.

Accept the silent thoughts and feelings

That are offered to you.

Clear my mind of the clutter of useless facts.

Bend down to me, and lift me in your arms.

Make me holy as you are holy.

Give me a voice to sing of your love to others.

Ancient Christian prayer, written on papyrus

No Waiting

Will tomorrow be less hectic and more inclined toward joy? Will I be less tired? God help me, I'm not waiting to find out. In your creation, joy can be found anytime, but mostly now. *Keep reminding me that* now *is all of life I can hold at any moment. It cannot be banked, invested, hoarded, or saved. It can only be spent.*

Darkest Before the Dawn

Teach us to know, God, that it is exactly at the point of our deepest despair that you are the closest. For at those times we can finally admit we have wandered in the dark, without a clue. Yet you have been there with us all along. Thank you for your abiding presence.

How good it would be if we could learn that God is easy to live with.

He remembers our frame and knows that we are dust. He may sometimes chasten us,

it is true, but even this He does with a smile, the proud, tender smile of a Father

who is bursting with pleasure over an imperfect but promising son who is coming

every day to look more and more like the One whose child he is.

Some of us are religiously jumpy and self-conscious because we know that God sees

our every thought and is acquainted with all our ways. We need not be.

God is the sum of all patience and the essence of kindly good will.

We please Him most, not by frantically trying to make ourselves good,

but by throwing ourselves into His arms with all our imperfections, and believing

that He understands everything and loves us still.

A. W. Tozer, *The Root of the Righteous*

Help Is at Hand

*Sometimes, Lord, the simplest ideas are wisest. When we wonder how to
  pray, the answer is readily "at hand":*
Thumb reminds us to pray for those closest: family, friend, neighbor;
Index for our guides, teachers, preachers;
Middle for leaders and those in authority;
Ring, the weakest finger, reminds us to pray for the helpless, sick, and poor;
Pinkie for ourselves.
*And so, O God, we come holding out our hands, knowing yours is
  outstretched and waiting.*

When I was a boy in my father's house,

still tender, and an only child of my mother,

he taught me and said, "Lay hold of my words with all your heart;

keep my commands and you will live.

Get wisdom, get understanding;

do not forget my words or swerve from them.

Do not forsake wisdom, and she will protect you;

love her, and she will watch over you."

Proverbs 4:3–6 NIV

At Home With God

Sidetracked, lost, and wandering far from the home of the heart,
I long to be at home with you. Home, not so much a place as a togetherness
where I am loved and welcomed just as I am, where I am sheltered, nourished,
equipped, and sent on my way. And to where, when I stray, I will be found
and returned. I get a glimpse of being at home with you, God, when I discover
I am being constantly nurtured by an ever-present Parent.

How Am I Doing?

All cats appear gray in the dark, Lord, and I have no clear sense of how well I'm doing.
I need feedback. Help me sort it into piles of what to keep, what to discard.
Remind me to offer feedback, for others look to me for
their validation; a simple "You're doing great" goes a long way.
I'm listening for your feedback, longing to hear, "Well done, good and faithful servant."

Letting Go

How blessed the one who can walk this journey
*   with a light grip on everything.*
For all will be released,
*   sooner or later.*
And I wish to practice now, Lord—
*   moment by moment*
*   —the letting go.*

God answers sharp and sudden on some prayers.

And thrusts the thing we have prayed for in our face,

A gauntlet with a gift in't.

Elizabeth Barrett Browning, "Aurora Leigh"

Lessons From the School of Life

So far, I have learned:

Silence speaks volumes when words dry up,
   and solitude never needs fearing.

Giving is clearly the best joy of all,
   and thankfulness: goal of all living.

Wisdom will enter with force unannounced,
   and grace goes wherever God is willing.

Relinquishing all—this is life's success.
   And seeking your purpose, the meaning.

Thank you, Master Teacher!

Longtime Friends

*Longtime friendship is a two-way mirror, O God, a gift from you
that returns our best selves reflected in the joy others get from just having
us around. Thank you for the gift of perseverance that keeps old friendships new.*

Lasting Legacy

Put off today and think of tomorrow.

How's that for a motto, Lord? Fine, for it invites me to forget past errors, ignore present "to-do lists," and look ahead.

What will I—family, friends, you—remember? That I did laundry instead of reading to a child or talking to a friend? What will endure? Time I gave committees instead of family and self? Chores I did instead of picnicking, walking, sitting on a log?

The answer prompts another motto, inspiration from you: Cherish the moment, celebrate today.

The Cure for Anger

O God, you see that when anger blinds the eyes
the truth disappears.
Give patience for rage, warmth in place of wrath.
And wrap all in the humility that comes from knowing:
They are all innocent in their own way.

Lost and Found:
A Sign of Hope to Follow

Daily stresses disorient me as completely as a red-winged blackbird,
herald of spring, lost in an unexpected snow.
I am found, Lord, when I see your fingerprint in the whorls of a fern unfurling,
lacy green and bold in the snow, and know that you are in charge
and endure, that you persevere and I, in you, can too.
Then I know I was never lost at all, just a bit off-course like a surprised bird.

Glorious Failure

It is good to know that adversity makes one wise,
  though perhaps not rich.
And that in great attempts at success
  it is glorious even to fail.

Near-miss Blessings

It's the close calls to body, mind, and soul that do me in, Lord, like crossing
railroad tracks only to see a freight train framed in my rearview mirror.
I'm keeping these moments in the margins of my heart to remind
me to live each day as found treasure.

Friend in Need

We enjoy too much the superior feeling of helping those in need.
Teach us, Lord, that it can be much harder to receive than to give.
And let us be humble enough to open our own hands, too,
when we're clearly in need.

Navigating Life's Rapids

*Like canoeists on the river rapids, O God, we've learned that
there is an easy way and a hard way to get through life.
Our days are as tumultuous as any rock-strewn river, and life is as
frightening as an unstable canoe:*

*Work—too much or too little. Age—too old or too young. Family—too near or too far.
Too little time and money but too much demand. Meanness and violence making us
hostages to fear. Stress, tragedy. Shifting values. A rock-strewn life.*

*It takes a guide and cheering family to make it through both life and river rapids.
The hard way, as you remind us, is alone. Cut off from you, cut off from others, we miss
the abundant life you promise. Yet running life's course as your child is as
life-changing as shooting river rapids. Both require moving into uncertain waters,
taking a chance on a guide we can't see, and listening for the
encouragement of those we can.*

*Come, God of wanderers and pilgrims, be our companion and guide.
Let prayer be a bridge, a meeting place spanning icy floodwaters.
We sense you near and are grateful to no longer be alone, knowing that
choosing to live relying on you as our guide is a move as major as
paddling onto the deepest, wildest river.*

*Steady us, for faith, like canoeing, isn't for sissies. It is a leap, a bold intention
to become forever changed by showing our trust in you. It is a loud, resounding
"Yes!" to your invitation:* Come, get in the boat, be fishers of folk, teach,
preach, heal; be my child . . . I will guide and go with you so you
don't have to flounder alone.

*Accepting it, we know that you will be first there when we tip
and that we need only listen to hear your directions.
We feel excitement building as we anticipate the journey.*

*There's an easy way and a hard way to do river rapids. To do life.
With you, O God, as guide, we joyfully move into the swift currents of life.*

Speaking Louder Than Words

Bless the words I am about to speak.
And help me remember, too, that true eloquence
does not consist of speech.
Let me attend therefore to my character,
for all I am speaks louder than anything I could say.

Prayer is one of the privileges of the child of God, made possible because Jesus Christ has opened up the way to our Father. God loves you, and He wants you to "not be anxious about anything, but in everything, by prayer and petition, with thanksgiving, present your request to God" (Philippians 4:6).

Billy Graham, *Answers to Life's Problems*

Guilty Conscience

Like a pebble in my shoe, a guilty conscience is blessing and curse, Lord.
It lets me fix what's wrong, but it can stop me in my tracks.
Help me take only my *guilt; to take more is to slow my progress by*
walking in shoes that don't fit.

Beautiful

You said that I am worthwhile and beautiful, Lord.
I hardly believed it
until one of your children—just this morning—
told me the same.

He who gives alms in secret is greater than Moses.

The Talmud

309

Goodness of God

*We spend a lot of time as prospectors of truth, digging, sifting, discarding
the world's "fools' gold" that is so lovely and enticing.
You, O God, are the genuine article.
Bless us with the power to go into our daily lives energized by this
truth and equipped to transform our searching world.*

As If It Were My Last

*Let me live my life from the viewpoint of my death, since I have been
moving toward it from the day I was born.
Remind me where I'm headed!
In this way, I know I can find new gratitude and
delight in each hour of the day.
For I can say: "This moment—right now—may be my last."*

Teach us, good Lord, to serve Thee as Thou deservest.

To give and not to count the cost:

To fight and not to heed the wounds:

To toil and not to seek for rest:

To labour and not to ask for any reward

Save that of knowing that we do thy will.

St. Ignatius Loyola, *"Prayer for Generosity"*

The Gift of Contrariness

Thank you, God of strong minds and stiff necks, for our bent toward contrariness.
Created in your image, we are your stubborn children and proud of it.
It takes a lot of backbone to stand tall these days.

When it comes to making life decisions, we don't want to be swayed by advice
that comes and goes like fads of fashion. We confess to temptation because
giving in and going along to get along are appealing.

Keep firm our resolve to be different; give us skills to handle teasing
and taunts and temptation. Bless our stubbornness, our insistence
from toddler days that "I can do it myself!"
In your guiding hands, we trust that it is good—even essential—to live contrary.
Thank you for the gift of intuition that bristles hairs on our
necks and leads us to say, "No way."

And as hard as it often is, we will trust and follow you, even if it makes us look
contrary. Sometimes, Lord, that simply means we are doing the right thing.

My son, do not despise the Lord's discipline

and do not resent his rebuke,

because the Lord disciplines those he loves,

as a father the son he delights in.

Proverbs 3:11–12 NIV

Father, I scarcely dare to pray,

So clear I see, now it is done,

How I have wasted half my day,

And left my work but just begun.

Helen Hunt Jackson, "A Last Prayer"

Extreme Love

You are everywhere, Lord, and we're comforted to be enfolded as we move through life's extremes. You are with us in birthings and dyings, in routine and surprise, and in stillness and activity. We cannot wander so far in any direction that you are not already there.

Eeny Meeny

I could flip a coin, Lord, and make a decision as sensibly as if I heeded advice being peddled. Experts expound on both sides of every issue, food to seat belts, and change their minds by tomorrow. Help me not do myself in by ignoring all of it! Moderation, Lord, moderation—I hear you.

Creative Thinking

Bless my mind today. I have some exciting thinking to do, and I know that all finite creativity springs from the Infinite Creator. Bless me, Mind of the Universe.

Different Is Lovely

We want to belong and go to great lengths to fit anonymously in, forgetting
we are like snowflakes, no two, thank God, alike. Each, snowflake and child of yours,
is the same in essence but different in form. Bless our unique, one-of-a-kind value.
We are heartened to know that no one is created more special. It is not your
way to be unnatural, to make one snowflake better than another.

For a Helper

As you launch out in this helping venture, may you continually recall that charity begins, but does not end, at home. That is why you are going.

When you seem to lose all your energy, when you've given all you can, rest in God's strength. When you come to the end of your rope, and patience seems to fly away, settle back in God's waiting arms.

Make times of peace and quiet for yourself!

And when you feel as though you'd like to quit and go home, persevere in the light of God's long-standing love for you over the years.

In all this hard work, rely not on your own willpower, but discover the blessing of being weak and in need. For this is the only way you will succeed, and it is the only way for others to have the opportunity to do something kind for you. Along with them—be blessed!

316

The text: Love thou thy fellow man!

   He may have sinned, One proof indeed,

He is thy fellow, reach thy hand

   And help him in his need!

Love thou thy fellow man. He may

   Have wronged thee—then, the less excuse.

Thou hast for wronging him. Obey

   What he has dared refuse!

Love thou thy fellow man—for, be

   His life a light or heavy load,

No less he needs the love of thee

   To help him on his road.

James Whitcomb Riley, "The Text"

Balanced Diet

In these nutrition infomercial, edutainment times, prepare me a table of pleasurable moderation. And, Lord of salads and sundaes, assure that nothing in your creation is itself bad; as always, it's what I do with it that determines its value. Be with me at the smorgasbord.

A Moment's Prayer

In my world of constant change and built-in obsolescence, may I take a moment to recall the everlasting nature of your promises.

Check It Out

It might be something, it might be nothing. Silly, silly us, ostriches with heads in the sand, we put off finding out. Remind us that the lives we gamble are gifts from you. Be with us as we check it out, check in, and check off worries that are probably nothing at all. Go with us as we find out.